The Kimberley

David McGonigal

Foreword by Tim Fischer

First published in 1990; reprinted 1992, 1993, 1997
First revised 1998
This revised edition published 2003

Published by Australian Geographic Pty Ltd
PO Box 321, Terrey Hills NSW 2084, Australia
Phone: (02) 9473 6777; Fax (02) 9473 6701

Managing Director: Rory Scott
Managing Editor, Books: Averil Moffat

First edition
Editor: David McGonigal
Principal photographer: Robbi Newman

This edition:
Principal contributor: David McGonigal
Text contributors: Hugh Brown, Nina Paine
Print production: Warren Field
Design: Maggie Cooper
Picture Research: Chrissie Goldrick, Warren Field
Cartography: Will Pringle, James Austin, Sue Dyhrberg
Editorial Assistant: Tina Miskelly

Specialist contributors:
Bob Young "An Ancient Land"
Kim Akerman "The Original Inhabitants", "Aboriginal Art"
Cathie Clement "European Explorers", "Early European Settlement"

Special contribution to photography for this edition: Hugh Brown

Text © Australian Geographic
Photography © Australian Geographic

Printed in China by Toppan Printing

National Library of Australia Cataloguing-in-Publication data:

McGonigal, David, 1950- .
The Kimberley.

Includes index.
ISBN 1 86276 052 7.

1. Aboriginal Australians - Western Australia - Kimberley.
2. Kimberley (W.A.) - Description and travel. 3. Kimberley
(W.A.) - History. I. Title.

919.414

■ Aboriginal children (left), enjoying the result of wet-season rains, make
the most of a natural rock diving platform on Glen Hill station.

■ Kimberley Dynamic rock art (title page) in some rock outcrops on the road to Mitchell Falls.

Foreword

In Australia there is inside country and there is outside country – and then there is the Kimberley. Inside country is generally regarded as being regions that are within 12 hours drive of any major capital city, outside country is more or less the balance, including the "great outback". However, the unique nature of the Kimberley, located the maximum possible distance from the heavily populated south-east – the Sydney, Canberra and Melbourne triangle – necessitates the special category.

In the 19th century serious consideration was given to building a transcontinental railway line direct from Sydney via Bourke, past Burke and Wills' "Dig Tree" near Cooper Creek, through Alice Springs, along the Tanami Track and ultimately to Collier Bay on the Kimberley coast. It would have been a great transcontinental line, longer than the east–west transcontinental Sydney to Perth, or the south–north transcontinental line Adelaide to Darwin. But it was not to be.

As it happened, economic downturn and war, in this case World War II, intervened. As well, the railway project had few champions, other than perhaps the Durack and MacDonald families. It reflects what is recorded accurately in this book – that the development of the Kimberley has been slow and not always steady, interspersed with a just few spectacular breakthroughs.

In the 20th century, between World War I and World War II, another proposal for the Kimberley was investigated. Inspections were carried out and debate held in the Western Australian State Parliament over the idea of creating a Jewish homeland settlement in the Kimberley. Again this was not to be as, among other hindrances, the Federal Government of the day did not back the plan, with the result that the Jewish home-state proposal reverted to the Middle East.

So, instead of the international airports, industries, freeways and traffic lights associated with intense development, the Kimberley at the start of the 21st century is an underdeveloped region of Australia: a sensational one of great natural diversity. This book helps conquer the barrier created by distance. Its expansive and detailed portrayal of the Kimberley cuts through to the beauty of this extraordinary place, from Argyle diamonds and the giant dam on the Ord River to the Bungle Bungle Range and the rugged Gibb River Road.

The Kimberley coastline, arguably one of the most dramatic in the world, and the captivating rock art of its indigenous people are unforgettable sights. And in this land of gorges and outcrops there's something special about the sunrises and sunsets too, whatever the season. The big bold reds of the rocks accentuate the Kimberley's giant, and ancient, landscape.

The compelling writing of David McGonigal and others who have contributed to this book, combined with the excellent photography and detailed maps associated with the high standards of Australian Geographic, create a renewed, vibrant invitation to visit the Kimberley. All aboard for the Gibb River Road, be it by train on the Ghan to Darwin and coach to the Kimberley, by sea to King Sound and Collier Bay or simply by air then a sturdy vehicle. There is a vast area of fascinating country to see and explore.

Tim Fischer

CONTENTS

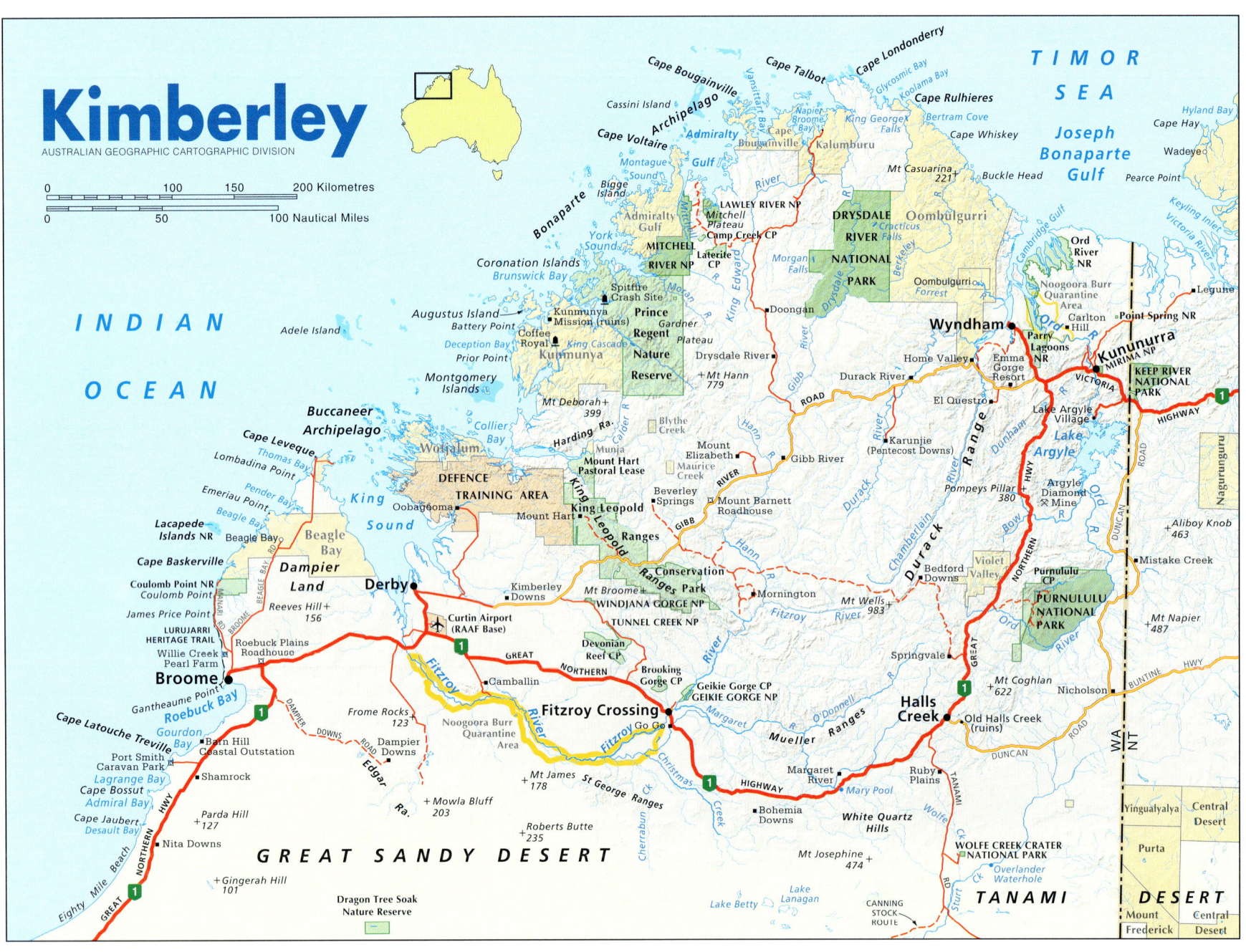

Kimberley

AUSTRALIAN GEOGRAPHIC CARTOGRAPHIC DIVISION

0   100   150   200 Kilometres
0   50   100 Nautical Miles

Introduction

We took off from Derby mid-morning and flew across King Sound towards the sea. As we turned north towards Kalumburu, the land and seascape that unfolded below us was awe-inspiring. Hundreds of craggy brown islands, some covering many hectares and others only a few square metres, were scattered across the sea in a maze that appeared to have been deliberately set for mariners. Where land and water met, there were empty beaches and rocky headlands; the outgoing tide left a line of foam as it swept towards the deep water, trailing eddies, whirlpools and whitecaps. Apart from the isolated mining

Stately brolgas (above) gather on the floodplains after rain, patrolling the shallows in a search for snails, insects and the roots of some swamp plants. The Kimberley is a wonderfully rewarding place for birdwatchers, particularly at the end of the wet season.

community on Koolan Island and the resort of Cockatoo Island, we saw not a single trace of human habitation during the five-hour flight. Elsewhere in the world, this scenery would attract thousands of tourists. But this is the remote Kimberley, so few even know of its existence.

Flying over the Kimberley affords a glimpse into the very essence of Australia. More than that, it's a glimpse of what the world was like when it was young. From high above, the twisted rock strata form intricate patterns, the original shapes of a now ancient land laid bare by millennia of erosion. There's no

predominance of mountains, rivers, forests, beaches, plains or grasslands. Rather, it's a mixture of all these, forming an integrated whole – the region called "the Kimberley".

The Aborigines of the Kimberley are the descendants of people who walked upon this land more than 40,000 years ago when Australia was still joined to New Guinea. They were here during the last Ice Age and had to move when the shoreline advanced 200 km into the Timor Sea and then receded as the world's oceans alternately froze into the polar ice caps and melted again. Today, there is a spirit of enthusiasm in the Aboriginal communities of the north-west as the original Australians develop a role in modern Australia which doesn't require them to renounce their ancient culture. This is reflected in a growing interest in Kimberley Aboriginal art.

The Kimberley is an enigma. It is one of the oldest parts of the most ancient continent on Earth, with a continuous population from not long after

the dawn of humankind, yet most of its European history is within living memory. Here, the first days of European settlement are not relegated to dry history texts: they are events experienced by the parents and grandparents of people living in the Kimberley today.

Although this is the part of Australia closest to our most populous neighbours (and was possibly visited by seafarers from Asia for centuries before any European vessel ventured to the east coast), it is regarded as the most isolated because it is the most distant from the main population centres on the eastern seaboard. Just arriving in the Kimberley feels like an achievement, yet the real adventure lies ahead.

It is this isolation that has allowed the Kimberley region to maintain a rugged individuality distinct from the rest of the country and yet it remains typically Australian.

The Kimberley is the north-west corner of the Australian continent. Its boundaries are the Timor Sea and the Indian Ocean to the north and west, and the Great Sandy Desert to the south. The eastern boundary is arbitrarily fixed as the Northern Territory border. Even so, the Kimberley region looks quite different from any part of the Northern Territory east of the Victoria River.

Mind-numbing statistics about the size of the Kimberley abound. With an area of about 421,000 sq. km, the region is slightly larger than Japan (377,708 sq. km) and much larger than the United Kingdom (244,100 sq. km), New Zealand (269,057 sq. km) or the

Large boabs (above), a familiar sight to all who know the Kimberley well, line the road into Mirima NP.

The broad Berkeley River has carved a gorge (opposite) through sandstone country as it flows north towards Joseph Bonaparte Gulf. Majestic rock walls like these are common in the Kimberley landscape.

State of Victoria (227,416 sq. km). Yet in this vast area there are only three towns with populations over 2000 and a total population of about 35,000. There's only one main road, the Great Northern Highway, and the section between Fitzroy Crossing and Halls Creek was the last part of Australia's Highway One to be tar-sealed. That was in 1986.

The region was named in 1880 by the Western Australian Government after the Earl of Kimberley, who was British Secretary of State for the Colonies at the time.

Until recently it was sometimes referred to as "the Kimberleys" and there was a strong demarcation between east and west Kimberley. There was a clear historical basis for this division. When continuous settlement of the area by white Australians first took place, some west Kimberley land was taken up by sheep graziers from the south of Western Australia and the eastern part was occupied by cattlemen from the eastern colonies, Queensland, New South Wales and Victoria. Soon afterwards the colony became self-governing and the east–west division was reinforced politically by the splitting of the region into two electorates. There was strong rivalry between the two regions that has only really broken down over the past 30 years with improved communication and the end of the Kimberley sheep industry. The last sheep station closed its gates in 1974.

Life in the Kimberley has always been hard. It is difficult to envisage the incredible courage and tenacity of those early pioneers – particularly the MacDonalds and Duracks, who arrived here in 1885 after several years droving their cattle from the eastern colonies. By settling the country's last major grazing area, those early pioneers were filling in the final piece of the picture of European Australia.

However, as in much of the New World, it was the lure of gold that brought the first large influx of Europeans (some 10,000 of them) to the Kimberley.

When the Kimberley goldfields (around Halls Creek) came to nothing in 1887, only two years after they were discovered, not everyone left. Those who stayed provided the nucleus for development and their towns continued to service the outlying population.

The history of the Kimberley has been one of slow consolidation rather than rapid development. That's not surprising in a part of the world where nature has been remarkably reluctant to give any encouragement to those presumptuous enough to seek a living from the land. The Ord River Scheme, first investigated in 1941, has yet to realise half its potential. As each new crop was tried, a new predator arose: magpie geese bred in astounding numbers to devour the rice crops, caterpillars ate the cotton and green vegetable bugs attacked the legumes. Only now are the farms of the Ord River Irrigation Area reporting the sort of ongoing success that will encourage others to take up the remaining land.

The distance from markets and the difficulties in reaching them has always plagued the cattle and sheep industries of the Kimberley. This is an area where it is almost impossible to travel during the several months of the wet season, far less move stock. Even when the roads are open, the closest Australian markets are at least 2200 km away in Perth or more than 3500 km away in the eastern centres of Brisbane, Melbourne or Sydney.

Even the first early runaway success, the Broome pearling industry, had its disastrous setbacks, like those caused by the cyclones of 1887 and 1910 which destroyed many luggers and killed their crews. But the indications are that the time of the Kimberley has arrived. Sydney was first linked to London by direct telephone in 1930, yet many homes in the Kimberley only joined the national telephone grid in the 1980s. The final sealing of the highway a decade ago removed a large psychological barrier for the traveller. Now tourists are arriving in unprecedented numbers

to see the wonders of this region. In a way, the remoteness and isolation that hindered development proved a boon because visitors now come to the Kimberley from the cities to seek the past. Broome's first renaissance since the decline of the pearling industry in the 1940s continues as its importance as a holiday centre grows. On the other side of the Kimberley, travellers pour into Kununurra on their way to see the newly World Heritage-listed Bungle Bungle Range, one of Australia's most intriguing.

There is also considerable mineral development throughout the Kimberley. The Argyle Diamond Mine, which began operation in 1983, extracts around 30 million carats of diamonds each year. That makes it the largest such mine in the world, producing about one-third of the world's diamonds. The restricted-access township for the high-technology mine looks like a huge tourist complex (complete with designer shade-sails over the swimming pool) near the foot of the Ragged Range.

Most people who visit the Kimberley develop a fascination for the countryside and the people who live here and want to return, and longstanding residents can't imagine living anywhere else. It's a truly beautiful part of the country that in many ways epitomises the image of Australia that Australians like to present to the world.

David McGonigal

Standing in isolation, the 385 m plug of Mt Trafalgar (opposite) is one of the highest points along the Kimberley coast. On the northern side of the mouth of the Prince Regent River, the massive bluff is a remnant of ancient sandstone beds.

AN ANCIENT LAND

More than anywhere else in Australia, the Kimberley is a region that calls upon us to examine the origins of our continent. In this region the bones of the land are exposed to even the most casual observer and it is a land of geological curiosities: fossil reefs and flooded mountains, flat-topped mesas (known locally as "jumpups") and sandstone spires, a desert meteorite crater and ancient folded mountains. These features are not interrupted by cities, small farms with planted crops or a dense cover of vegetation. The modern visitor is granted an uncluttered view; here the land is all there is.

Geological evidence suggests that the Earth and other planets were created 4600 million years ago. This figure, like so many in geology, challenges the limits of human comprehension but, flicking through millions of years like the days on a desk diary, a fascinating picture emerges of how today's landscape came about.

The oldest rocks in the Kimberley were formed around 2000-1900 million years ago and, apart from some younger ones on the southern margins of the region, virtually all Kimberley rocks are more than 400 million years old. To put that in perspective, until 200 million years ago all the world's landmasses were part of a single supercontinent called Pangaea (meaning "all lands"). About 150 million years ago Pangaea split into two large continents known as Gondwana and Laurasia. The Australian continent resulted from the break-up of Gondwana about 100 million years ago.

If it were only the rocks of the Kimberley that were so old, Australia would have no claim to the title of oldest continent – many parts of the world have rocks of similar antiquity. But the Kimberley, and much of Western Australia, are special because there has been very little geological activity since most of the rocks were formed. Not only are the rocks themselves ancient but the landscapes cut from them have barely changed in millions of years.

The last period of intense mountain building in the Kimberley was a staggering 1700 million years ago. Few of the rocks that were formed 500-400 million years ago show signs of subsequent deformation. That makes them very old indeed when you consider that The Himalaya, which was formed when the Indian subcontinent moved gradually north and collided with Asia, is only 4 million years old. Even the oldest parts of the ocean basins are only 100 million years old. When compared with the mobility of most of the Earth's crust, Australia is indeed a timeless land.

Ridges and hills dominate the landscape as you look up Piccaninny Creek towards the Bungle Bungle massif (opposite). Virtually unknown until the 1980s, the Bungle Bungle Range 40 km south-east of Warmun Community is one of the fastest developing areas of tourist interest in WA. In 2003 it became part of a World Heritage Area when Purnululu NP was listed.

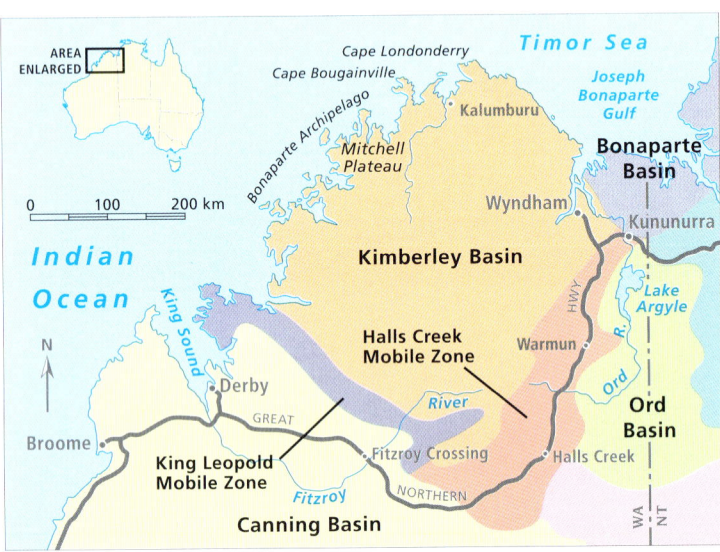

The geological zones of the Kimberley region (above).

Elaborate concentric banding (opposite) in fine-grained sandstone from Mount Jowlaenga quarry bears a close resemblance to an Aboriginal ochre painting.

Geological areas

The Kimberley is made up of five geological areas (the Kimberley, Ord and Bonaparte Basins, and the Halls Creek and King Leopold Mobile Zones) and is fringed by one more (the Canning Basin). The heartland is the Kimberley Basin, an enormous raised thickness of sandstones, shales and basalts, which have been subjected to only minor faulting and warping since they were formed between 1800 and 1650 million years ago.

The King Leopold and Halls Creek Mobile Zones, or orogens (an "orogen" is the eroded remnant of mountain belts), on the flanks of the Kimberley Basin are areas of intense folding and faulting. The sedimentary and volcanic rocks of these zones were altered greatly by the heat and pressure of mountain-building forces and great masses of granitic rocks have risen from deep in the crust. However all this happened in the distant past, about 1800 million years ago.

Sediment eroded from the older rocks was swept into several large basins (the Ord and Bonaparte Basins and the Canning Basin), around the orogens. The limestones and sandstones made from those deposits have been carved into the spectacular landforms for which the Kimberley is renowned and these basins are the parts of the region with which most travellers are familiar. They also contain the Kimberley's best cattle country – especially on the great basalt plateaus and plains of the eastern part of the Ord Basin.

Today it is hard to imagine the hot, arid landscape of the Kimberley buried under glaciers. However, it was, in two glacial ages 700 and 600 million years ago, at a time when the whole continent was much further south than it is today. There is clear evidence of this in Moonlight Valley to the east of Warmun Community and also in the Charnley and Lennard river areas in the western part of the Kimberley. Here, very large boulders have been transported almost 50 km from the nearest outcrop of the same rock. In Moonlight Valley there are polished rock fragments and pebbles with the distinctive grooving of glacially transported debris.

Fossil reefs, visible in several parts of the Kimberley today, reveal some fascinating aspects of the history of this land. By 400 million years ago the continent had moved north: the Kimberley was in the tropics and much of the lowland was underwater. Remnants of that time, some of the best fossil reefs in the world, are to be found on the edge of the Canning Basin. Today the reefs appear as narrow limestone ranges rising 100 m or so above the surrounding plains. The best known is the Napier Range, especially where the structure of the ancient reef is beautifully exposed in the walls of Windjana Gorge. Geikie Gorge provides a similar cross-section of the ancient reef. Another, but less spectacular, fossil reef is the Ningbing Limestone, which is about 50 km north of Kununurra.

The changing climate

The climate was far from stable in those ancient times. Glacial deposits in the Grant Range, near the lower reaches of the Fitzroy River, show that very cold climates prevailed again about

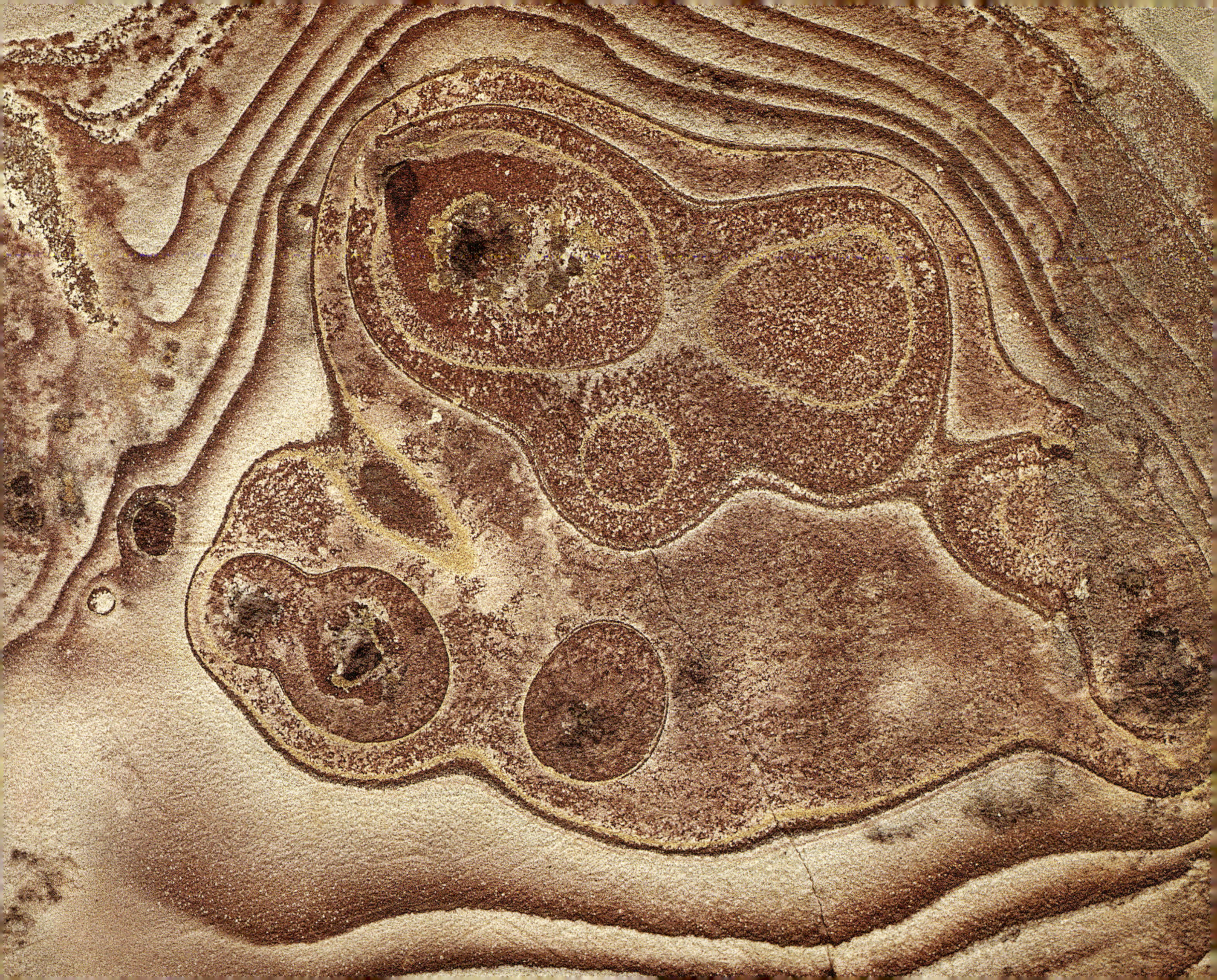

Fluctuations in sea level, shown in the map above, have been extensive over the past 100,000 years. This is the Greater Australian landmass above sea level about 20,000 years ago.

Nestled between Roebuck Bay and the Indian Ocean, Broome (above right), known as the "Port of Pearls", is the only Kimberley town with a beach. However, until 6000 years ago, the site of Broome wasn't even on the coast. During the last Ice Age, 20,000 years ago, the sea-level was 100 m lower and 200 km further out than it is today.

250 million years ago. But over the past 100 million years, the Kimberley climate has been consistently warm to hot. The most spectacular evidence of this is at Gantheaume Point near Broome, where the footprints of a warmer climate reptile, the dinosaur, have been perfectly preserved in sandstone for about 100 million years.

Until about 30 million years ago, the climatic conditions in the region were a great deal wetter than they are today: there is fossil evidence of widespread rainforests. However in another reversal, the sand dunes along the southern edges of the Kimberley are evidence of very dry conditions in the near past, within the last few hundred thousand years.

The last very dry spell was only about 20,000 years ago and, at that time, with much of the water of the planet's oceans trapped in large polar icecaps, the sea was more than 100 m below its present level. The very broad and shallow continental shelf of the Timor Sea was not under water then, so the shoreline was 200 km further out than it is today. The dry conditions and shift in the shoreline resulted in a considerable shift in the distribution of the Aboriginal population.

The most recent melting of the polar icecaps and the consequent rising of the sea flooded a vast area of lowland beyond the plateau escarpment that today forms the spectacular northern coastline of Western Australia. The numerous long inlets along the coast are drowned valleys and the many offshore islands are the tops of hills that once rose above ancient lowlands.

■ Dubbed "China Wall" by the local community and bearing a passing resemblance to its namesake, this natural rock wall 6 km from Halls Creek is part of what is claimed to be the longest quartz reef in the world.

Falls tumble into the Lennard River Gorge (above). During the dry season the flow is moderate but the wet-season deluge causes a dramatic increase in volume. The effect of erosion of the landscape over tens of thousands of years is shown clearly here. Flow along the streambed cuts down the underlying rocks, and flow over the falls causes the face of the waterfall to retreat upstream.

Mineral riches

The orogens are the Kimberley's main sources of mineral wealth. The Halls Creek gold rush of 1885-1886, the iron ore mines of the islands of Yampi Sound and, from 1988 until its final closure in 2001, the lead-zinc mine at Cadjebut, have all made a contribution. But the Argyle Diamond Mine south of Kununurra in the east Kimberley has been the most dramatic development of mineral resources in recent years. The west Kimberley was explored for diamonds in the late 1960s but that exploration was unsuccessful.

The rocks of the Kimberley Basin may also be the basis of major future development: in the northern part there are large fields of bauxite formed by prolonged tropical weathering of basalts in the area. And, for energy resources, the main prospect is in offshore reserves of gas north of both Broome and Wyndham.

Drainage patterns

A curious feature of the Kimberley is the striking contrast between streams draining to the north and those draining to the east and south.

Northerly streams like the Drysdale and Mitchell are straightforward: they flow towards the sea from high areas in the centre of the Kimberley. Their course is governed by underlying geological features. The Charnley River, for instance, follows the boundary between very resistant sandstone and more easily eroded volcanic rock.

The Prince Regent River is a particularly striking example of a river responding to the structure of the landscape. It flows straight as an arrow for more than 100 km along a great fracture in the King Leopold Sandstone. Its tributaries flow in at clearly defined right angles, their courses guided by smaller fractures that intersect the main one.

Where the northerly streams cross from one rock type to another, the level of the stream bed may change abruptly, resulting in a series of cascades. The Mitchell River makes an even more spectacular shift as it plunges in a series of waterfalls over the edge of the Mitchell Plateau.

By comparison, many of the streams draining to the Fitzroy and Ord rivers in the east and south display a remarkable independence of geological controls. The Hann River cuts straight through some of the highest ridges in the region to join the Fitzroy, which itself cuts first through the sandstones of the King Leopold Ranges and then the limestone ranges at Geikie Gorge.

The Ord River, too, cuts through major ranges, notably the Carr Boyd and Dixon ranges. The Margaret River slices through a major topographic barrier, the King Leopold Ranges, even though there appears to be a much easier pathway across lower ground around the edge of the ranges. In fact, of the streams draining this eastern side of the Kimberley, only the Chamberlain River shows strong geological guidance: it flows straight across the outcrop of soft shales exposed beneath the upturned edge of the King Leopold Sandstone of the Durack Range.

Why do the rivers of the south and east shun the easy route? In many cases, the answer is that their courses were established when the features visible today were buried under masses of sediment washed down from the main Kimberley block into the Canning Basin. The ancient forerunners of rivers like the Lennard and Fitzroy had an unimpeded passage across the sheets of sediment sloping gently to the southern lowlands. When the rivers cut down to expose the rocks that are the hills of today they had the time to carve through them as they were slowly exposed, so maintaining their courses. This is how the spectacular gorges of Geikie and Windjana were created.

The creation of river valleys through the high barriers of the Carr Boyd and King Leopold ranges was a variation on this. The ancient rivers flowed across broad plains. These plains were then slowly uplifted. The rivers still cut across the rising landscape but

The world's largest diamond mine and the principal source of deep-pink diamonds, Argyle Diamond Mine (above) is also unusual geologically. Argyle diamonds are found in a volcanic rock called lamproite. Before the Ellendate and Argyle pipes were found in 1976 and 1979 respectively, it was believed that diamonds were only present in the rock known as kimberlite (which takes its name from the city of Kimberley in South Africa). The Argyle discovery has opened new areas of diamond exploration worldwide.

as they cut through the strata of different hardnesses, they stripped away soft rocks and left harder ones standing as ridges.

Shaping the landscape

The most striking feature of the Kimberley is the shape of its mountains, a result of the incredible time span in which the basic characteristics of limestone and sandstone were left undisturbed to be shaped by erosion and weathering.

Limestone is very strong mechanically but chemically weak. Because of its mechanical strength it is able to stand in vertical or even overhanging faces but it is readily dissolved by the very weak organic acids formed by the mixing of water with decaying vegetation. The result is majestic sheer faces such as those of Geikie and Windjana gorges, and limestone outcrops fretted with small pits and channels. The dissolving of limestone by water has also produced many underground caves and, especially where the roof of a cave has collapsed, steep-sided depressions. These processes are visible at Tunnel Creek where the stream drains a depression on the edge of the Napier Range through a long cave.

Sandstone normally exhibits exactly the opposite characteristics to limestone: it is chemically very strong but mechanically weak. The most curious feature of all the Kimberley landforms is that caves are found not only in the chemically susceptible limestones but also in strongly cemented quartz sandstones, among the most chemically resistant of all rocks.

Some caves occur near the summit of the Cockburn Range, west of Kununurra, but the most outstanding example is "Whalemouth Cave" in the Osmand Range east of Warmun Community. This is 220 m long and 120 m deep and, unfortunately, not accessible to the public. Its name is apt – the exit is 60 m high and 45 m wide!

The reason for this unusual characteristic and resulting landforms is the region's geological stability. When these sandstones were formed, the pressures within the bedding fused the individual grains of sand together. Groundwater generally can't penetrate this cement but, given time, it can seep along joints and fractures, eventually dissolving the cement and washing away the sand. These fractures widen into long, narrow caves. Although the process may have been faster in the distant past when the climate was wetter, today it is infinitely slow.

The Bungle Bungle Range in Purnululu National Park, which was declared a World Heritage Area in July 2003, is a spectacular sandstone formation that owes its existence to different causes. In its sandstone, the "cement" between the grains of sand never completely filled the gaps. This allowed water to flow through the rock and eventually wash away all the cement. But even without the bonding, neighbouring interlocking grains support each other. The result is that the rock is mechanically very strong when compressed but very weak when pulled apart. Bungle Bungle Range sandstone can support a weight of 40 megapascals (almost

Ranger-in-charge Bob Taylor and visitor Rob Thompson stand deep within a cleft on the western side of the Bungle Bungle Range (above). Although the ancient sandstone has lost most of the "cement" that originally bonded it, individual sand grains are interlocked, giving it the stability to form cliff faces.

Like a coral reef after someone has pulled the plug ... That's a fair description of the scenery at Geikie Gorge (opposite). Kimberley limestone ranges such as the one bisected by the Fitzroy River at Geikie Gorge are excellent examples of fossil reefs. Cyanobacteria and other lime-secreting organisms were the reef builders – not corals. The white discolouration marks the flood level of the river in the annual wet season.

■ Derby (above) stands on a low, flat peninsula jutting into the mudflats of King Sound. The highest point in town is only 20 m above sea-level and the demarcation line between permanent vegetation and tidal marshes occurs at an elevation of 6 m or less. King Sound is the mouth of the Fitzroy, May and Meda rivers. It has a tidal range of 10 m, a treacherous entrance and extensive shallows.

6000 pounds per square inch) but crumbles away when even lightly struck. This allowed water erosion to carve up the range but what remained was able to stand alone as steep-sided towers, ridges and gorges.

One of the most notable features of this landform is its surface of horizontal black and orange tiger stripes. Surprisingly, these are less than one centimetre thick – underneath there's white sandstone. The skins consist mainly of clay and silica. They are orange where small amounts of iron are present, but black where lichens and micro-organisms cover the surface. If it were not for these skins, which protect the rock surface, rates of erosion would be much greater.

As a finishing touch to this landscape, the Bungle Bungle Range was probably hit by a large meteorite at some time in the distant past. The crater itself has been almost entirely levelled by erosion and today it is only a shallow depression. The most lasting evidence of the impact is that the rock around Piccaninny Gorge has been heat strengthened. Here the sandstone doesn't fall apart grain by grain but collapses along fractures to form huge cliffs.

The Bungle Bungle Range is not unique; similar structures exist at the Ruined City in Arnhem Land and in the Sahara Desert as well as nearby at Kununurra's Hidden Valley and across the Northern Territory border at Keep River National Park. However, the Bungle Bungle Range is much larger and is the best example of its kind in the world.

About 100 km north of the Bungle Bungle Range lies the Ragged Range, a complex of conglomerate and sandstone towers. In part, the scenery is like that of the Bungle Bungle Range but without the beautiful symmetry.

At the northern foot of the Ragged Range there is a huge, solitary, enigmatic dune, standing some 200 km from other desert dunes south of the Kimberley. The sand had undoubtedly been blown from streambeds but the age of the dune and the conditions under which it formed have only recently been determined. It is now believed that the dune began to accumulate during an arid period about 22,000 years ago and sand has accumulated again during the last 6000 years. Stream deposits close to the foot of the dune have been dated and show that about 40,000 years ago, and again between 12,000 and 6,000 years ago, rainfall was considerably higher than it is at present. The dune and its surrounds have therefore provided important evidence of climate change in the region.

Majestic cliffs

While towers, domes and pillars are characteristic of many of the sandstones in the Ord and Bonaparte basins in the eastern part of the region, the much older sandstones in the Carr Boyd and Cockburn ranges and in the heartland of the Kimberley Basin have been carved into great cliff lines. These sandstones, generally tightly cemented, collapse in great slabs along vertical fractures rather than grain by grain.

Where the sandstone bedding is almost horizontal, as in the Cockburn Range, the landscape is dominated by flat-topped plateaus. Flat-topped mesas, as they are known, bounded

"Tiger-striped beehive mountains" clamoured the first media reports of the Bungle Bungle Range (below). However, the beauty of the contrasting bands is only skin deep - below lies uniformly white sandstone. The banded skin, less than one centimetre thick and easily broken, is part of the reason why the Bungle Bungle Range has survived - it inhibits the process of erosion. The orange bands are composed of clay and silica and the black band is organic growth, mainly lichens, established wherever the silica skin shatters.

■ As the walls of "Cathedral Gorge" glow in the midday sun (above), the huge cavern at the base of the cliff dwarfs the crouching figure of Rob Thompson examining the clear waters of a pool crowded with tiny frogs. This intriguing composition of red rock, white sand and crystal water is the headwater of a small, unnamed tributary of Piccaninny Creek, the main watercourse of the southern Bungle Bungle Range.

by cliffs standing above debris slopes are also common throughout the central part of the Kimberley Basin, especially around the Barnett Range.

Along the northern edge of the Mitchell Plateau there are grand sandstone cliffs that drop sheer to the plains below. In the regions around Halls Creek and the Margaret River, flat-lying sandstones and laterites form caps on low mesas.

Where the rocks have been tilted, the main landforms have cliffs on one side and long slopes on the other. In a particularly picturesque turn of phrase, geographers refer to these as "hog-backs". There are numerous examples of these, especially on the Bandicoot and Carr Boyd ranges. In the more remote Moonlight Valley (on the northern side of the Osmand Range) the tilted glacial beds have produced layer upon layer of resistant outcrops forming a series of cliffs that descend northward like a giant inclined stairway.

But pride of place must be given to the Elgee Cliffs, an array of scarps and tilted benches running northwards for 125 km along the Chamberlain River. The Elgee Cliffs, which are off normal tourist routes, except at their northern extremity, are one of the most outstanding landforms in Australia. They are best seen from an aircraft, and from this perspective they stretch to the horizon in a single, unbroken escarpment.

The rugged Kimberley landscape, with its rocks, gorges and ancient mountains, has a grandeur second to none. It has been shaped by the erosion of diverse rock masses over enormous spans of time. The geological time scale of the Kimberley reduces the probable 40,000 years of human occupancy to a scant moment.

The stamp of ancient times is still clearly evident throughout the Kimberley, in direct contrast to the rapid changes typical of more mobile parts of the Earth's surface. The slower tempo of change in the Kimberley region has produced a unique landscape.

■ Towering over the plains of the Pentecost River, the cliff line of the Cockburn Range (below) resembles the walls of a fort. These ramparts are made of strongly cemented sandstone lying in flat, horizontal beds that break apart as blocks to produce vertical cliff faces dropping to steep scree slopes below.

"OF DROUGHTS AND FLOODING RAINS"

I was leaning against my four-wheel-drive in Wyndham when the weather report came on the car radio. It was April and the regional forecast for the Kimberley, as usual, was "scattered showers". There wasn't a cloud in the sky and none was to appear during the day. A truck driver standing nearby mirrored my thoughts: "That was a lot of use, wasn't it?" he declared. "A piece of land much larger than England and it's covered in one sentence. Won't rain here but they might catch a bit more over in Broome."

It is understandable that the news broadcasters dismiss the Kimberley in a single sentence: the whole area supports fewer people than a regional town elsewhere. Looking at the Kimberley on the map, one tends to think of this remote, empty region as one homogeneous region but it isn't. The title of this chapter comes from a line in Dorothea Mackellar's poem *My Country*. It is certainly apt for the Kimberley. There are two general categories of Kimberley climate. Like the Northern Territory north of Katherine, the area within a band running along the coast from the mouth of King Sound to a point north of Wyndham has a "hot, moist climate with a marked dry season in winter". The rest of the Kimberley is categorised as having a "dry, hot climate where winter is drier than summer".

As the map on page 28 indicates, there are wide-ranging differences in rainfall throughout the Kimberley. By far the highest rainfall is in the area around the Mitchell Plateau in the remote north-west and the lowest is, not surprisingly, along the fringes of the Great Sandy Desert. The record highest rainfall for the Mitchell Plateau was 2154 mm in 1973: Balgo Hills in the Great Sandy Desert recorded just 90 mm of rain in 1958.

Throughout the Kimberley the monsoonal rains of the tropics are vital. The rains may leave stations and communities isolated for months on end but they provide the fodder and stored water to see them through the seven or eight dry months. An 1838 surveying expedition was the first to note the dramatic effect of Fitzroy River flooding. The river drains an area larger than Tasmania and the sailors noted flood debris 7 m up riverside trees, signs of a strong contrast to the quiet dry-season river.

However, in some years the "wet season" provides very little rain (often coinciding with El Niño events) and stock must be sold off or they could die. Better management of stocking levels and stored fodder can reduce the effects these days but it's hard to counteract events

Storm clouds gather over Cable Beach, Broome (opposite), and the afternoon sky darkens. As the dry season draws to an end the clear dry weather gives way to a cycle of daily thunderstorms. Humidity is often high at this time and the weather can be trying but the wet season, which it heralds, is usually welcome. The torrential rain of the Wet revives a parched land.

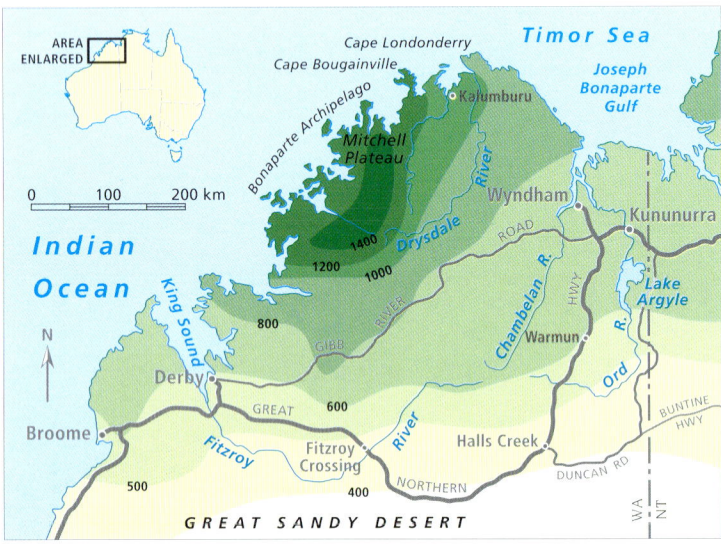

Average rainfall in the Kimberley, shown in millimetres in the map above, varies greatly across the region.

such as the two years between 1951 and 1953 when the east Kimberley received a total of just 308 mm rainfall. In 1972-1973 the north Kimberley recorded two of its driest years but they were followed by heavy rains to compensate. Those making their living from the land have learned to provide for such possible extremes of climate.

Although the temperatures throughout the Kimberley region generally conform to the "hot summer and cool winter" pattern, there are significant variations between towns. Derby and Broome, for example, don't experience the top temperatures of Wyndham or Kununurra but they generally have higher humidity and don't cool off as much overnight. Halls Creek, the Kimberley township that lies furthest inland, has less rain and less humidity, as well as generally cooler nights, than the others. If the effect of humidity and temperature are combined into a discomfort index Derby may be one of the most uncomfortable places in Australia to spend summer.

Unlike the broad division of seasons into "Wet" and "Dry", which most Kimberley residents recognise, the distinctions developed by Aboriginal people are much finer. The different Aboriginal groups in the Kimberley divide the year into five to nine seasons, depending on the specific climate of the area in which they live.

Aboriginal people are prepared to equate their seasons to the dates of the Gregorian calendar but the seasons they recognise relate to the span of natural events rather than fixed dates. The seasonal determinants may be climatic – such as the advent of the south-east winds marking the beginning of the cold season. But seasons may also be marked by more subtle indicators, so a coastal group will know that when a certain plant is in flower they will be able to find the eggs of nesting turtles.

Just as the English word "winter" has a wealth of connotations, each Aboriginal season has innumerable markers. So summarising the Aboriginal cycle of seasons is, by necessity, simplistic. However, even in the simplest form it provides a fascinating insight into a way of life inextricably linked to the land and the seasons.

One dialect of the Wunambal group lists seven seasons:

Wundju (January-February): the wet season. Plants are scarce and animals hard to hunt because of the weather.

Mayaru (February-March): the weather is better and food crops are still growing.

Bandemanya (April): crops are maturing and much more food is available.

Goloruru (late April): the trade winds begin.

Yirma (May-August): the cold, dry time. A rich time when roots, fruit and seeds are abundant and the grass can be burnt off to herd kangaroos towards hunters. The south-west winds begin. Enough food can be stored to allow gatherings of Aboriginal groups.

Yuwala (September-November): hot and dry. Rivers are drying up and most root crops have been gathered.

Jaward (November-December): the build-up to the wet season with thunder and lightning. Some fruits ripen, replacing the last root crops.

Like other rural areas, the Kimberley is dominated by the seasons. The rain that closes roads often puts airstrips out of action too, so people don't get around much in the Wet (from November–December to March–April). Station work almost ceases and many Aboriginal workers take part in gatherings and ceremonies at this time.

The tourist season starts about April and continues until the humidity and heat become too uncomfortable. The clear days and good driving conditions attract a large number of people who are keen to explore – and to enjoy camping out. This dry season is also a busy time for the rural industries. Towards the end of the year there's tension in the air as large thunderclouds develop each afternoon only to dissipate overnight without rain. One employer told me: "Every staff complaint I've ever received came in the weeks before the Wet." With a cloud-burst, the monsoon season arrives. The amount of rain that falls to replenish the parched land sets the pattern of Kimberley life for the following 12 months.

The dry season often brings bushfires to the Kimberley and vast areas may burn unrestricted (above). Frequently fires are the result of lightning strikes and are part of the cycle of climatic events. Many birds take advantage of the fires to feed on the swarms of insects flushed out by advancing flames. Driving becomes a more hazardous experience when fires fill the air with smoke. It's essential to take extra care.

Cyclones

Cyclones, those irresistible forces of destruction against which we are powerless, exert a fascination that draws us in just as objects are drawn into the eye of the maelstrom. For anyone living outside the cyclone belt, there is a shiver in contemplating what it's like facing the mightiest engines nature produces. But for those who live there, a cyclone is just a random and dangerous fact of nature.

The Kimberley coast is a cyclone area and one of these storms may arrive at any time between November and April. A tropical cyclone is a body of very strong winds rotating around an "eye" of extremely low pressure. Australian cyclones rotate clockwise while those of the Northern Hemisphere (where they are generally known as typhoons or hurricanes) spin anticlockwise. A cyclone is likely to have a diameter of over 320 km and, near the eye, wind gusts may reach over 200 km/h.

Although the part of the West Australian coast most prone to cyclones is around Port Hedland, the Kimberley near Broome has seen its share and, in the days before cyclone warnings, they often resulted in great loss of life. A cyclone that struck the pearling fleet at Eighty Mile Beach in April 1887 was first reported to have left 30 vessels and 500 men missing although the final count was 22 vessels sunk and 140 lives lost. Only nine years earlier, in March 1878, a cyclone had destroyed two ships loading guano at Browse Island with the loss of 22 lives.

The township of Broome was worst hit by the cyclone of November 1910. Many buildings were destroyed and the pearling fleet, which was caught on the way to shelter, lost 26 vessels and about 40 men. In late March 1935, the pearling fleet (already hit hard by the Great Depression and low prices for mother-of-pearl) was at sea when it was struck by a particularly vicious cyclone: 21 of its 52 vessels were sunk and more than 140 men died.

Today, using satellite cloud photographs and radar, meteorologists normally declare a "cyclone watch" if one looks likely to strike a coastal community in 24 to 48 hours, and a "cyclone warning" if the threat is more immediate – within 24 hours.

That was the system in effect when Tropical Cyclone Rosita crossed the coast 40 km south of Broome just after midnight on 20 April 2000. It is rare to have a cyclone so late in the wet season but Rosita was something special. It had first been noted as a low in the Timor Sea five days earlier and was graded as a category 1 cyclone on 18 April. The following day it had intensified to category 5 – the highest. Category 1 cyclones may have wind gusts up to 125 km/h and are regarded as having minimal damage potential. Category 5 is a hurricane with winds in excess of 280 km/h and, not surprisingly, extreme damage potential. Rosita was still category 5 when it hit the coast. Broome's maximum wind gust was 153 km/h, causing extensive damage to trees; power was cut in some parts of town for several days afterwards.

Eco Beach Resort, south of Broome, took the full brunt of the cyclone. It had been designed and built to withstand cyclones – but not ones that could fling a five-tonne

■ "Weather balloons are filled with hydrogen and make a hell of a mess if they explode," says Andrew Duncan, meteorological officer in Halls Creek. "Static electricity is the principal hazard." After a balloon is launched (opposite), the observer climbs into the device alongside the launch site and tracks the balloon on radar, recording wind direction, temperature and humidity data. Balloons expand as external air pressure decreases – most burst below an altitude of 26,000 m.

■ The morning after the storm. The damage to Eco Beach Resort (inset below) is a vivid indicator of the wind's amazing force. Tropical Cyclone Rosita caused extensive damage here when it struck in the early hours of the morning on 20 April 2000. The dark skies of cyclone season are common here between December and April.

The dramatic spiralling cloud bands of Tropical Cyclone Inigo are captured in this satellite image (right) of the Timor Sea region on 5 April 2003. With estimated winds of up to 240 km/h, this was one of the strongest cyclones ever known in the West Australian region. Inigo caused extensive damage in Indonesia but it weakened before reaching the Australian coast. The occurrence of cyclones in the Kimberley is usually no more than one every three years and although coastal communities are at risk, cyclones weaken as they move inland where their accompanying rains are welcome.

shipping container some 700 m and throw some buildings into others. At nearby Yardoogarra Station a caravan blew away and disintegrated and a semitrailer was blown onto its side. The station owners took shelter in a brick and steel outbuilding and watched the brick walls bulge under the onslaught of the wind.

To the hapless observer, the first effects of a cyclone are wind, rain and rising seas. At the peak of the cyclone's fury, there are shrieking winds and torrential rain. If the eye of the cyclone (which is usually 20 to 30 km across) passes overhead, the wind stops suddenly and there may even be blue skies. The return of the storm is equally immediate with winds at full strength from the opposite direction for several hours, tailing off over several more.

Tropical cyclones need to draw energy from the sea so they decay rapidly once they move inland. Towards midnight on that same day, Rosita was 700 km inland near Balgo Hills in the Great Sandy Desert. Even then it was still a cyclone, with enough intensity to cause some damage to the community.

Anyone living in cyclone-prone areas – and people planning to visit during the storm season – have it in their own interest to familiarise themselves with safety measures and emergency procedures. It is not reassuring to learn from a Bureau of Meteorology publication entitled *Surviving Cyclones* that cyclones in the Australian region exhibit more erratic paths than cyclones in other parts of the world ". . . movement in any direction is possible including sharp turns and even loops". Just one month before Rosita, Tropical Cyclone Steve started north-east of Cairns and crossed Queensland, the Northern Territory and the Kimberley before re-strengthening out to sea west of Broome and heading down across the Pilbara coast and Carnavon. Finally, Steve was no more than a rain-bearing depression that passed over the goldfields and Esperance to exit into the Great Australian Bight.

▦ Life-giving water: the permanent waterholes and billabongs of the Kimberley, such as this one (above) north of Kununurra, are home to an incredibly wide variety of plant and animal life.

▦ Many roads are impassable and river crossings are out of the question during the wet season, but as the rains abate (left) and the waters recede, travel conditions improve.

THE ORIGINAL INHABITANTS – THEN AND NOW

One of the most remarkable highlights of Australian history was the arrival of the first people in Australia. It is thought that this took place more than 40,000, possibly as much as 60,000 years ago and the details of those first Australians have been obscured by time. But archaeologists have pieced together clues that provide a framework for modern theories.

Modern Aboriginal people are believed to be descendants of people who travelled down through the arc of land that is now the Malay Peninsula, and the Indonesian Archipelago. This was during the last Ice Age when much of the ocean was bound up in the polar icecaps and sea-levels were much lower than they are today. The fall of the oceans resulted in the emergence of a land bridge linking Australia with New Guinea, but there was never a direct land link between Australia and South-East Asia. The combined landmass of New Guinea and ancient Australia is known as Sahul.

There were times when the Kimberley coast was separated from Asia by less than 100 km of sea and those living across the water would have been able to see smoke from naturally occurring bushfires started on the north-west coast of Sahul by lightning. By observing signs such as the distant smoke and the habits of migratory birds, people living in Timor would have been aware that land existed to the south. It may seem surprising that humans 50,000 years ago had the ability to build vessels and an urge to venture across the sea; but they did. Much earlier peoples had probably reached the island of Flores in central Indonesia using watercraft. It is thought that these early vessels were probably rafts made from bamboo. And it was strictly a one-way trip in these craft: bamboo has a limited life and there was no indigenous bamboo or other suitable timbers for raft-building with the simple stone technology used by early people in Australia. Once here, the migrants were probably unable to make craft suitable for a return journey.

Waves of settlement

These first settlers almost certainly didn't arrive as a single group. There were probably many landfalls along the coast between the Kimberley and the exposed Timor and Arafura plains over thousands of years. It is likely that the first peoples to occupy the coast of Sahul first populated the country by moving along the coast and up major river systems, never moving far from water.

Dappled by the sunlight filtering through coconut palms, a young Broome cyclist pauses in a suburban street (opposite). More than 40 per cent of the population in the Kimberley is made up of Aboriginal people. Many visitors to the region, from elsewhere in Australia and also from overseas, are drawn to the region by the opportunity to view the unique Aboriginal rock art.

AREA ENLARGED

Timor Sea

Cape Londonderry
Cape Bougainville

Murrinh-patha

Miwa
Gamberre   Kwini
Wilawila

Kalumburu

Joseph Bonaparte
Gulf

Doolboong

Wunambal

Indian

Ocean

Winyjarrumi
Yawijibaya

Yiiji
Munumburru
Guwij   Wyndham

Wolyamidi   Miriwoong
Kununurra

Gajirrawoong

Worrorra

Ngarnawu
Worla
Walajangarri

Ngarinyin

Lake
Argyle

Bardi   Jawi
Nyulnul   Umiida
Unggarrangu
Jabirrjabirr
Nimanburru
Ngumbarl
Broome   Jukun
Yawuru

Andajin

Kuluwarrang
Warmun   Kija

Malngin

Warrwa
Unggumi

Ord   R.

Bunuba

Derby

Fitzroy
Crossing

Fitzroy   River

Halls Creek

Nyikina   Gooniyandi

Nyininy
Jaru

Wanyjirra

GREAT SANDY DESERT

Karajarri

Mangala
Juwaliny   Walmajarri

INFORMATION COURTESY
OF DR WILLIAM McGREGOR

WA   NT

0   100   200 km

N

The map above shows where the different Aboriginal language groups occur in the Kimberley.

Later generations spread throughout Australia and archaeological sites from 40,000 BP have been found in the south of the country – on the Swan River, WA, and Lake Mungo in western NSW. The earliest Kimberley sites to have been discovered (in the Napier Range and at Yampi Sound and Collier Bay) reach back over 40,000 years and on the Ord River, near what is now Lake Argyle, vestiges of human habitation from 21,000 years ago have been discovered and carbon dated. The first parts of Australia settled are not those that today are yielding the oldest archaeological finds. The reason for this is that today's coastline was established only about 6000 years ago. The first settlements would have been at the mouths of the great river systems: the Fitzroy, King Edward, Drysdale, King George, Ord, Victoria and Daly. But the coastal lowlands of those days would now be 150 m under the sea and up to 250 km offshore.

Early animal life

The country in which the new arrivals found themselves appeared very strange. The animals were mainly marsupial and quite unlike the Asian creatures with which they were familiar. Kangaroos 3 m tall, an ancient relative of today's wombat that was the size of a rhinoceros, a leopard-sized marsupial carnivore and goannas up to 6 m long were some of the more bizarre inhabitants. Thylacine and Tasmanian devils also lived in the northern part of the mainland at this time. The diet of the early Australians in the Kimberley appears to have remained consistent (at least over the past 18,000 years) and included shellfish, fish, lizards, reptiles, including crocodiles and turtles, marsupials such as kangaroos, bandicoots and possums and birds and their eggs, as well a wide variety of plant foods. Nectar from flowers, sugar secretions found on some leaf-scale insects and honey gathered from the hives of native bees or in arid regions from the bodies of certain types of ants provided an element of sweetness in the diet.

European contact

By the time the first European settlers arrived on the east coast the Kimberley population had a highly developed social structure. Some 31 different languages, belonging to six distinct language groups were to be found in the Kimberley. The early European settlers, who had great difficulty pronouncing Aboriginal words, tended to dismiss the languages as "primitive". In fact, Aboriginal languages have extensive vocabularies and grammar at least as intricate as those of English and other European languages. Like German, Aboriginal languages tend towards single words built up to say what would take a phrase or sentence in English. Without a written language, there was a great dependence on oral traditions and complex song cycles were composed in which the indigenous concepts of the cosmos and the laws that governed both the human and the natural world were transmitted. In some areas a complex iconography, or system of visual symbols, was created in order to illustrate the oral traditions that lay at the heart of the religious and social life of the area.

Language and cultural groups

There is a clear demarcation line between languages of the north and south Kimberley. The line runs from Thangoo station on the coast, along the southern edge of the Canning Basin to Nicholson station, then to Timber Creek in the Northern Territory. Languages north of the line predominantly use prefixes and those to the south suffixes. This distinction reflects great differences between the cultures of the north and south Kimberley, particularly in the complex rules governing marriage. Location also played a vital part in determining the pattern of life, which varied greatly. The Wunambal and Worrorra people alternated between the coast and rugged inland, travelling along the river valleys, while the Bardi were "saltwater" people, never far from the sea, who exploited the offshore reefs and islands. Along the Fitzroy River, the Nyikina utilised the river and the floodplains, while upstream, the Bunuba lived in the rugged limestone of the Oscar and Napier ranges.

Living together

An extensive trade route linked all the groups of the Kimberley and, ultimately, those of adjacent areas and beyond. These trade routes were known as the "Winan" in east Kimberley and "Wunan" in west Kimberley. The "goods" varied from everyday utensils to ceremonial objects or religious songs. Objects were held for only a short time before being passed down the line. So pearl shell from Dampier Land has been found near Adelaide and boomerangs from the desert would be used as ceremonial clap sticks by Wunambal people who didn't make or use boomerangs themselves.

There were fights and battles between groups but these were to resolve conflicts, not for conquest. Conquest is impossible when no land can be won. Each clan was regarded as holding an area of land in trust and no battle could take that right away. The link between the people, religion and land is not one that can be severed. Aboriginal people are bound to the land by ties which extend back to beings who roamed the land (or arrived here from across, or out of, the sea) during the period known as the "Dreaming".

The dislocation of Aboriginals as a result of European settlement was great because the land was (and remains) such an integral part of the Aboriginal identity. At first there were skirmishes with explorers and trailblazers but when the pastoralists and graziers moved in and the Kimberley gold rush occurred, there was strong motivation to completely usurp Aboriginal rights to land in the Kimberley. Aboriginals were in demand as a cheap (often unpaid) source of labour, working as pearl shell divers and shepherds. Conflicts over access to land and resistance to forced labour, as well thefts of stock, resulted in many of the indigenous people being killed. It is impossible to estimate how many were killed (and diseases such as measles, smallpox and flu introduced by immigrants also took a heavy toll) but we can say that many more indigenous people were killed than Europeans. Despite these conflicts, Aboriginal labour played a vital part in the success of the Kimberley's primary industries.

The story behind this 1919 photograph (below), taken in the east Kimberley, is unknown, though its main subjects are, at the very least, living a semi-traditional lifestyle. The grass-and-bough shelters and sparse vegetation point to the shot being taken during the dry season, and the robust physiques, good looks and self-confidence of the north-west peoples noted by some early European observers are clearly evident.

An Aboriginal stockman (below) from remote Pentecost Downs station uses his all-purpose hat to take a drink from the Durack River during a hard-earned break. Long hours in the saddle under a tropical sun ensure Kimberley station work remains one of the hardest jobs on the land. With their understanding of the land and ability to deal with the often harsh conditions, Aboriginal stockmen and station hands have played a vital role in the development of the Kimberley.

A number of Aboriginal groups died out in the first 100 years of European settlement of the Kimberley. In 1979, it was estimated that six languages and dialects had disappeared and four more were spoken only by the elderly. Many other groups moved away from their traditional lands, often to the towns, where they were forced to adopt a language (mainly English) in which they could converse with Europeans and the Aboriginal people of other groups living there. Today there is a concerted effort to record the languages still existing and to encourage the use of those where there are significant numbers of fluent speakers.

Times of change

Ironically, one of the most disruptive influences on Aboriginal life in the Kimberley was one that was intended to be beneficial. Until 1968, many Aboriginals stayed on or near their traditional lands by affiliating with stations in the area. The lease owners could support many Aboriginal workers because most were "paid in kind", receiving food and other supplies in lieu of wages. The Pastoral Act, which came into effect in 1968, ensured that Aboriginal workers received award wages, and this, coupled with a fall in meat prices, led to this source of employment almost ceasing and many Aboriginals being forced into towns.

Although it is doubtful if she said it, Daisy Bates (who visited the Kimberley in 1900) has long been associated with the phrase "to smooth the dying pillow" because she regarded the Aboriginal people as a doomed race. It took most of the 20th century to remove the destructive force of the rationale behind this epithet. Since the late 1970s there has been a reaffirmation of Aboriginal pride, noticeably lacking, or concealed, since Aboriginal people were severed from the land.

Towards the end of the 1970s a series of events pushed Kimberley Aboriginal affairs into the national spotlight. In 1977, following the Western Australian State election, accusations were made that the Liberal Party had used unfair means to influence the Aboriginal voters in the Kimberley. The Court of Disputed Returns found that Aboriginal people had been misadvised by Liberal scrutineers and a new election was called. As a result of this new election, the sitting Liberal Member lost his seat.

Kimberley Land Council

During 1978–1980, events on Noonkanbah station increasingly became front-page news around Australia. The first confrontation arose when an oil company's bulldozer driver desecrated a sacred site at Noonkanbah station while the inaugural meeting of the Kimberley Land Council (KLC) was taking place there. Three years later, the dispute culminated in the oil company being instructed by the Western Australian Government to carry out a test drilling on a sacred site. The drilling rig required a police escort from Perth to Noonkanbah. After drilling, the company reported that no oil was found. But the die was cast: from now on the Aboriginal people's political voice would continue to be heard.

The KLC became that voice of the Aboriginal people of the Kimberley although, as more Aboriginal corporations have developed the confidence to be self-reliant, it is no longer the sole representative. Further, many corporations are tackling the problems they see within their communities and resolving them. The KLC is, however, of importance, assisting Aboriginal groups in the Kimberley to have their traditional ownership of land and sea recognised.

Australia is coming to realise the worth of the Aboriginal contribution to the nation: the understanding of the environment, the rich cultural traditions and the great merits of Aboriginal art. The Kimberley, with a population that is approximately 40 per cent Aboriginal, plays an increasingly important part in developing a long overdue understanding of the first Australians. Indigenous groups now run tourist ventures and indigenous contemporary music, theatre and art of the Kimberley are important economic as well as cultural assets, recognised not only regionally but also in the international arena.

■ Traditional owner and native title applicant Richard Hunter gives evidence to Federal Court judge Ron Merkel during the on-country hearing of the Rubibi native title claim in Broome in 2003. The KLC has provided assistance to many such applicants

Irish-born Daisy Bates (above) maintained her strict dress code even when most inappropriate for the conditions at Beagle Bay and Broome. The evocative expression "to smooth the dying pillow" may not have been used by this journalist and social worker/researcher, but it well mirrors her work with what she considered a doomed race and became a catchphrase during decades of indifference to Aboriginal people.

The mission at Kalumburu (right) was first established in the 19th century and is now an active community of Aboriginal people. The thriving orchard and vegetable gardens are an important contribution to self-sufficiency in this isolated spot.

Kimberley missions

A priest from Scotland, Father Duncan McNab, established the first Kimberley mission at Cunningham Point (north-west of Derby) in 1885. The indigenous people there, having been exposed to "blackbirding" raids and pearlers, remained wary of the priest. In 1887, Father McNab fell ill and withdrew. Less than a year later, the abandoned mission burnt down.

In 1890, Bishop Matthew Gibney of Perth (McNab's supervisor) enlisted the help of several French Trappist monks to start a mission further west at Beagle Bay. The monks established a branch at Disaster Bay in 1896 and, five years later, they handed control of both places to the Pallottine Pious Society of Missions. The Sisters of St John of God then arrived to help and, in due course, the two orders also established missions at Lombadina, Balgo and at Lagrange.

While Beagle Bay Mission initially aimed to assist Aboriginals already affected by the impact of European settlement, new missions started to take Christianity to others. These included Forrest River (Oombulgurri), Pago (Kalumburu) and Port George IV (Kunmunya).

A government land grant to the Church of England led to the establishment of an Anglican mission at Forrest River in 1897. The local Aboriginals fought the missionaries and

the Church withdrew its people in 1898. It tried again in 1913 – this time with staff from Central Africa living in a fortified compound on the old site – but its aims were achieved only after experienced Australian staff arrived.

Sydney Hadley, a hard-bitten pearler and beachcomber, "got religion" and worked at Forrest River Mission with two Aboriginal men from Sunday Island (in King Sound) in 1898. The following year, assisted by the last of the original Forrest River missionaries, he established Sunday Island Mission. He received government subsidies but his unorthodox methods, which included undergoing ritual initiation and becoming involved in Aboriginal-sanctioned relationships with indigenous women, made it difficult for him to muster church support for the mission. When the Australian Aborigines Mission took over Sunday Island in 1922, it adopted a far more conservative approach and many Aboriginals left for the mainland. Twelve years later the mission followed them to a site near Cockatoo Island. That proved unsatisfactory and the mission moved back to the island in 1937.

In 1908, the New Norcia Benedictines leased land near the top of the Kimberley at a place called Pago and established the Drysdale River Mission. Despite initial animosity and an Aboriginal attack in 1910, the Benedictines persevered, acquired more land and, in 1932, opened a road from the Gibb River-Wyndham Road to what is now Kalumburu. The road has never been developed, even by outback standards, and is still a difficult one to travel. the mission is quite isolated during the wet season. Two RAAF runways were built nearby in 1940 and the airforce stationed personnel at the Drysdale airfield in 1941. The adjacent Truscott air base, which housed Australian, US, British and Dutch personnel, was completed after the Japanese bombed the mission. The wrecks of several aircraft (US, British and Dutch) can still be seen near the runway at Kalumburu.

The first Presbyterian mission in the Kimberley was established in 1912 on a lugger moored in Port George IV. It was under the direction of Robert and Frances Wilson who then built a house at the port. Three years on, they determined that the site was unsuitable and the mission moved to Kunmunya. There, the fortunes of the residents fluctuated according to the seasons. By the end of the 1940s the vitality of Kunmunya was so badly eroded that the Worrorra Aboriginals agreed to accompany the Presbyterians to a new site. They moved to Wotjulum and then, in 1956, to Mowanjum near Derby.

Other missionary activity, which began with the arrival of Tom Street in Derby in the late 1920s, involved the United Aborigines Mission (UAM). Staff from UAM later established missions at Fitzroy Crossing and Halls Creek.

Much of the history of the interrelationship of races in the Kimberley has been either in the work of the missions or in the strictly commercial areas of the pastoral industry or, specifically around Broome, the pearling industry. There is no doubting the good intentions of the mission workers. They did, however, face considerable opposition over the years and, even now, with the mission era finished, people continue to debate the pros and cons of its impact on Aboriginal people.

■ The Sacred Heart Church at Beagle Bay was designed by a German father from the Pallottine Pious Society of Missions. Its completion in 1918 was the grand culmination of several years of toil in which the mission's Aboriginal residents worked tirelessly with the missionaries, cutting timber, making thousands of clay bricks, and collecting shells that were burnt to make the lime plaster. They also collected mother of pearl shell and opercula (a rare stone taken from shellfish) that decorates the unique altar and other parts of the church.

ABORIGINAL ART

The most famous figures in Kimberley rock art have long been the images of the Wandjina found in many caves of central and western Kimberley. Wandjina are titanic anthropomorphic creator beings, which reveal themselves to humans as monsoonal storm clouds marching across the Kimberley landscape during the wet season. The paintings of Wandjina have stolid, staring, mouthless faces – eerie, with an other-worldly air about them. As well as the Wandjinas themselves, other images in this monumental style include Rainbow Serpents, yam(s), hives of wild bees, goannas, crocodiles, tortoises, kangaroos and emus. There are also petroglyphs, or rock engravings, relating to the exploits of the Wandjinas in some areas. Wandjina art is believed to be relatively recent, perhaps several thousand years old.

Over the past decade or so, paintings in an earlier style of rock art known as Kimberley Dynamic figures or Bradshaw paintings or, to use the Ngarinyin term for them, *Gwion-Gwion*, have attracted the attention and study of scientists and other interested people. The fine fluid lines that characterise much of the elegant solid-figured images of the *Gwion-Gwion* art were drawn by birds using their beaks, say the Aboriginal peoples whose territory this is. Motifs include humans, fish, reptiles, marsupials and birds. This art form has been found to be at least 17,500 years old. While most images appear to have been painted in a single colour (red, or mulberry), it is apparent that some styles at least incorporated several colours. These other colours,

usually white and yellow, are less durable than the iron oxides that provided the red pigments and so usually disappeared over time.

While paintings in these two styles, Wandjina and Kimberley Dynamic, are well known, they are generally restricted to one area of the Kimberley. Overall, the Kimberley region embraces five artistic zones. The map on page 44 shows where these zones lie.

Zone I (A), which takes in a large part of the western and central Kimberley, is the area where Wandjina and Bradshaw or *Gwion-Gwion* rock art is to be found.

The Wandjna paintings are believed to have been done by the great creator beings that still exist as the paintings or in trees and landforms. Mortals can draw spiritual sustenance from them and senior clansmen can reaffirm the continuity of life by regularly retouching the paintings (also an expression of ancestral bonds). If the retouching is done at the appropriate season, it activates the dormant powers of beings that maintain the natural cycles of the cosmos.

Spiritually important Wandjina figures, owl-like ancestral beings, dominate the work of Aboriginal artists in the north Kimberley (opposite). These slate carvings, on sale in Wyndham, came from Kalumburu. Increasingly, interest in Aboriginal art is encouraging people to travel to remote parts of the Kimberley to view the rock art that, in some cases, is more than 10,000 years old.

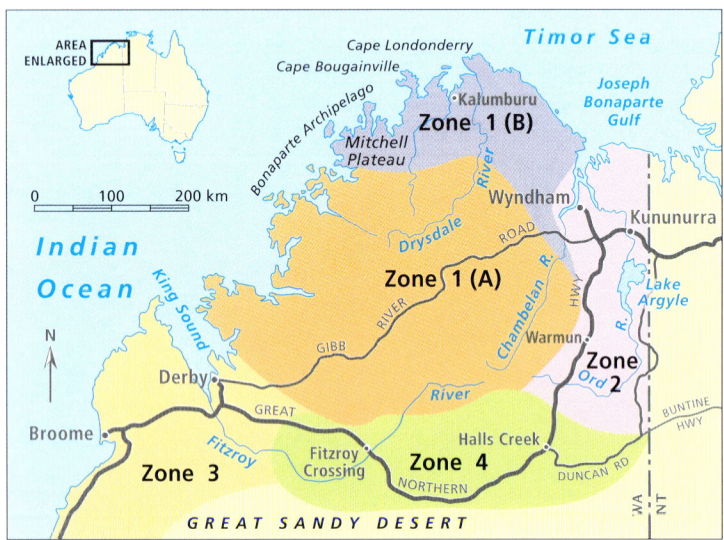

It is possible that Kimberley Dynamic paintings originally had a much wider general distribution; several have been found in the Keep River area of the Northern Territory. The geology of the area west of the Ord Basin generally consists of more friable rocks and it is likely that most traces of early art have long since eroded away. Apart from the rock art, weapons and utensils were decorated with figures of Wandjinas and snakes, or with animal and bird tracks. Dancing ornaments consisting of large thread-cross emblems, often with the thread-work arranged about a large semicircular painted panel, are a feature of the public *Palka* dances of both this area and Zone 1 (B).

Zone I (B) in the northern Kimberley has few Wandjina paintings but probably the greatest number and some of the most spectacular Kimberley Dynamic figures to be found anywhere in the Kimberley. The latter are not only extremely well preserved, but many paintings also show what appears to be elaborate ceremonial behaviour involving several or more individuals. Study of Kimberley Dynamic paintings in this region provides a unique glimpse into ancient Aboriginal life here. Unlike Wandjina rock paintings, these were not, apparently, retouched by later artists. The Kimberley Dynamic paintings show a level of extraordinary sophistication only matched in Australia by the Dynamic Figure art of Arnhem Land in the Northern Territory.

■ The different art zones of the Kimberley region are shown in the map above. Travel to some of the remote locations is difficult and slow, but Aboriginal rock-art sites attract a growing number of visitors each year.

■ Dynamic figures from the north and central Kimberley (right) are the most elegant of the many rock-art styles found in WA. This art style provides many clues to the dress, ornaments and hairstyles worn by ancient people – clues that are otherwise lost in time.

One of the most important aspects of this general art style is that, unlike the more recent Wandjina art, humans are often depicted bearing weapons or elaborate handbags, decorated with a wide range of ornaments and often showing complex hairstyles. Another important aspect of this style is that there are a number of distinct subsets within it; by examining the order in which they are superimposed one on the other, it is possible to determine their relative chronological sequence. This provides some insight as to when different types of

Vibrant colours and intricate design (below) characterise much of Kimberley Aboriginal art. The style dates back to antiquity but the materials may be very modern — this painting has been done with acrylic paint on masonite.

■ Carving on pearl shell (above). Pearl shell engravings, many with complex patterns, from the Kimberley coast were important articles of indigenous exchange. They have been found as far away as western Queensland, in Central Australia and along the Great Australian Bight, SA.

weapons and utensils came into or fell out of use in the past. In the early phases of the style the boomerang appears to be a weapon of considerable importance. It is replaced at a later time by a focus on multi-barbed spears, thrown without the aid of a spear-thrower. Neither boomerangs nor barbed spears were made or used by the people of Zones 1(A) or 1(B) in historic times. Today the Wandjina and Kimberley Dynamic rock art styles provide the thematic grounding for the production of paintings on both bark and canvas, at Mowanjum and Kalumburu, the two major art centres associated with this area.

Zone 2 includes the Ord Basin and extends into the Victoria River Basin. There are rock paintings here in solid colours outlined with fine dots, usually of white ochre. Motifs include fish, reptiles, birds, marsupials, vegetable foods and humans. "Lightning Man" type images, each holding one or more stone axes in their hands, or chains of men and women each linked to their neighbour at hand and foot like cut-out paper dolls, are also found. The complex ceremonial exchange routes that link this region to the peoples of the Victoria River, Fitzmaurice River and Daly River systems provide a milieu of cultural continuity of myth and ritual that is also to a degree reflected in the rock art.

More recently one art tradition, painted boards carried on the shoulders of dancers, has been translated into one of the most dynamic art movements to have developed in Australia. Initially derived from the works of artists painting boards for a dance cycle known as the *Krirr-krirr*, this style of painting was to develop into a school of art often referred to as the Turkey Creek or East Kimberley School of Indigenous Art. The style is unique to the region, portraying the country itself – in both plan and profile. Previously Kimberley paintings (unlike those from other areas) depicted beings and objects rather than places. However, unlike the highly schematised portrayals of landscapes common in the desert country and east and central Arnhem Land, the Kimberley representations are characteristically uncluttered.

Zone 3 extends south beyond the Kimberley. In the Kimberley section rock art is rare and limited to a few areas where petroglyphs (rock engravings) occur. On the other hand there is a rich tradition of woodworking and especially the carving of pearl shell. Also, wooden artefacts and ornaments and emblems of pearl shell were both skilfully carved and engraved. Motifs include parallel meander, interlocking key and herringbone designs. More recently naturalistic motifs occur – including scenes of contact with Europeans. The zigzag motif is associated with water; ripples on the otherwise smooth surface of the sea, as the tides ebb and flow, the wind brushing the surface of lake or river, or floodwaters ably demonstrating the power of the Rainbow Serpent. Mazes, infilled with careful crosshatching, and interlocking key patterns represent the travels of ancestral heroes and the landscapes they passed through or created. Combining such significant water motifs with pearl shell, whose flashing nacreous surface was believed to be the embodiment of water itself, was to create an object whose significance was to be revered over more than half the continent.

Another art form closely associated with Zone 3 are complex thread-cross emblems called *ilma* that are used in public ceremonies on the Dampier Land Peninsula. Combining thread-cross work with painted two-dimensional sculptural forms, these dance emblems represent islands, tides, reefs and whirlpools, storms and other natural phenomena, as well as artefacts and events alluded to in the ceremonies at which they are presented.

Zone 4 covers the basins of the Fitzroy, Mary and Margaret rivers. It is an area rich in rock art and is a mixture of the painting traditions of the central Kimberley, Ord and Western Desert. Rock engravings are far more common here than elsewhere in the region. Simple engravings depicting concentric circles, "tally marks" (rows of short parallel lines), or animal tracks frequently occur. More complex works include the "knight in armour" of Sturt Creek. Unfortunately the significance of much of the engraved art has never been properly recorded. Some works have been identified as records of the creator beings themselves, others mark the ceremonial designs ordained by the creators. Animal and bird tracks may possibly illustrate creation stories of the region or possibly hunting magic. Some are known to have been used in children's games.

There is some evidence that the traditions of the Wandjina painters were spreading south into this region at the time of European settlement. The Fitzroy River, however, flowing between the Great Sandy Desert to the south and the Kimberley Plateau to the north, was itself such a rich and fertile area that it permitted cultural interchange on a grand scale to take place. Ceremonial gatherings in the Fitzroy Basin brought coastal, desert and the stone country people of the plateau together for both economic and religious purposes. As the original inhabitants of the Fitzroy Basin and the people of the ranges reeled under the impact of European settlement, desert-derived cultural activity strengthened as people from the Great Sandy Desert region drifted north to stations and towns in the southern Kimberley. As with the other areas, this zone now supports a vibrant contemporary indigenous art community based at Fitzroy Crossing.

Aboriginal art today

In the last 20 years the Kimberley has moved from a position where indigenous cultural attributes were seen primarily to have been grounded in the rock art, particularly that associated with the Wandjina beings, to being a major producer of contemporary art of an international calibre. Unlike many other areas in Australia, no one style or format has come to dominate the region as respect for cultural sensitivities are maintained between the various tribal groups. Notwithstanding the forces of tradition there is continual experimentation and innovation that ensures that the Kimberley region produces and will continue to produce some of the best and most sought after art in the nation.

A number of Aboriginal communities, tourist operators and pastoral stations provide tours of selected rock art sites and/or other cultural experiences. It is best to check locally or with accredited agents to arrange visits. In most major centres and Aboriginal communities there are galleries or art centres where purchases may be made or where visitors may meet local artists.

From bark paintings of Wandjina figures to mass-produced T-shirts, Waringarri Aboriginal Arts shop in Kununurra (above) carries a range of Kimberley commercial Aboriginal art forms. Catering to an ever-growing market for Aboriginal arts and handicrafts, Waringarri and similar shops in Broome and Fitzroy Crossing are operated by local Aboriginal communities, each favouring work by local artists.

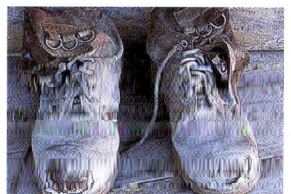

EUROPEAN EXPLORERS

Although Captain James Cook was the first European to explore the east coast of the continent, he certainly didn't discover Australia. Before he first set foot on Australian soil in 1770, people had visited the north-west corner of the continent for hundreds, perhaps thousands, of years. The first arrivals were the Aboriginals (at least 40,000 years before anyone else), and they came to stay, but some scholars consider it possible that Chinese and Arab traders visiting Indonesia also came south and made at least brief contact with the Kimberley coast in the centuries before the first Europeans landed there.

By the 19th century, Indonesian fishermen were regularly sailing to the Kimberley coast to collect trepang (also known as sea-slugs or sea cucumbers) between January and May each year. They gave the Kimberley the name Kayu Jawa (which means literally "wood of Java"). Most of their activities took place southwest of Cape Londonderry (near Kalumburu). Because they boiled and dried the trepang before transporting it, the fishermen established shore camps near fresh water and inevitably came into contact with the Aboriginal people. Such early liaisons may account for the "light-skinned Aborigines" reported in 1838 by Alexander Usborne, master of HMS *Beagle*, and by George Grey who led an overland expedition south from Prince Edward River. Another indication that people from Indonesia probably visited the coast is the presence of tamarind trees, native to south-east Asian regions, along the north coast of Australia.

Early visits to the coast

The European credited with the first definite contact with the coast of what is now Western Australia is the Dutch captain Dirk Hartog, who visited the coast in 1616. He was sailing the *Eendracht* from the Cape of Good Hope and was bound for Java. The first recorded exploration of the Kimberley coast was conducted in 1644 by another Dutchman, Abel Janszoon Tasman (after whom Tasmania, which he also visited, is named).

Tasman's 1644 visit is not well documented. Journals recording his voyage, which he undertook on behalf of the Dutch East India Company, have disappeared and only scanty details survive elsewhere. Our main record of Tasman's remarkable achievement is a chart based on his work in mapping the north coast of Australia from Cape York to North West Cape. It was this chart that named the land "Compagnie Nieu Nederland" (later generally adopted as "New Holland") and contributed many of the Dutch placenames along the coast of northern Australia.

Rough and difficult country (opposite) often greeted the early explorers who struggled to investigate the Kimberley on foot. Alexander Forrest (1849-1901), explorer, surveyor and entrepreneur (inset), was the individual most responsible for opening up the region. He reported the Nicholson Plains to be "the finest part of Western Australia that I have seen".

■ Like this portrait (above) by an unknown artist, lifelong adventurer William Dampier (1651-1715) was a shadowy, romantic figure. His first view of the Australian continent was of the Kimberley coast near the Buccaneer Archipelago while he was a crew member of the one-time privateering vessel *Cygnet*. He was not impressed. He returned to the Kimberley in 1699 in command of HMS *Roebuck*.

■ Dressed in their best (above right), Abel Janszoon Tasman (1603-1659), his second wife, Jannetie, and his daughter by his first marriage, Claesjen, posed for artist Jacob Gerritz c. 1637. In two remarkable voyages, Tasman discovered New Zealand and Tasmania in 1642, then charted the coast of northern Australia in 1644. His voyages set the stage for Dampier's exploration of the north coast and Cook's journeys through the western Pacific.

We do know that 25 men from the three ships under Tasman's command landed on the Kimberley coast, probably to the north of Roebuck Bay, and received an apparently hostile reception before a volley of gunfire drove the indigenous people away.

It was the Englishman William Dampier, however, whose two visits to the Kimberley coast are best recorded, and his is the best known of the early European contacts with what came to be called Australia. On his first visit in 1688 he was aboard the *Cygnet*, a one-time privateering vessel, looking for new trade routes and opportunities.

Although Dampier had been a privateer, his colourful and much-publicised reputation as a buccaneer is unproven, and was not applicable to the *Cygnet* voyage in any case.

The *Cygnet* was beached for careening and repairs probably north of what is now Cygnet Bay. The crew, who needed food and drinking water, approached some Aboriginal people to seek assistance but they fled. However, by Dampier's account, the Aboriginals were friendly enough once they had lost their initial fear. They donned cast-off clothes and ate the European food offered to them but declined to work for the mariners.

Dampier's description of Aboriginals as "the miserablest people in the world" is well known. He was less than flattering about the land, too: "A dry sandy soil, destitute of water except you make wells." However, it should be noted that this was in January, possibly in advance of the monsoon rains, and that he was nowhere near a river. Dampier's impressions may have been different if he had arrived elsewhere on the coast.

Dampier's major achievement was as a comprehensive (and colourful) diarist. He was the first Englishman to write about Australia. After his return to England he published *A New Voyage Round the World* in 1697, which was an instant success and made him famous. His next nautical appointment was as a captain in the Royal Navy in command of the 290-ton, 12-gun, HMS *Roebuck*. His job was to explore the coast of New Holland then known only for its west coast. He sighted the coast in August 1699 and entered Shark Bay before proceeding north. Reaching Lagrange Bay, he went ashore on the universal quest of all early mariners for fresh water.

This time, Dampier's contact with Kimberley Aboriginals was less satisfactory than his first encounter. After a skirmish that left casualties on both sides, he obtained some brackish water from a well near the beach. He sailed the *Roebuck* for Timor and later investigated the coast of New Guinea. Dampier's exploits are commemorated by Kimberley placenames that include Roebuck Bay, Cygnet Bay, the Buccaneer Archipelago, Dampier Land and, further south, by the Dampier Archipelago. Most of these names were given by Phillip Parker King many years later.

On both voyages, Dampier's observation, collection of specimens and recording of detail were excellent. In 1699 he noted the presence of pearl shell on the Kimberley coast, little realising that, in another 200 years, that shell would be traded on the international market.

In the late 18th and early 19th centuries several French explorers visited the region, adding a great many French names to places around Australia's coast.

Phillip Parker King

Phillip Parker King's maritime surveys conducted between 1818 and 1822 included the Kimberley coast. King's surveys were aimed at charting that part of the Australian coast not covered by Matthew Flinders (that is, the area from Cape Leeuwin, WA north to Arnhem Land). While examining the north-western coast between the Gulf of Carpentaria and North West Cape, King hoped to find a major river flowing from the interior of the continent.

During the four dry seasons King spent working on the Kimberley coast (exploration was only possible during the dry season), he discovered Cambridge Gulf (the outlet for the Ord River) and examined the outer reaches of the sound that now bears his name (and is the outlet for the Kimberley's other major river, the Fitzroy). At Port Nelson he found water was plentiful one season but non-existent the next. In contrast, the Prince Regent River yielded an abundant and reliable supply, and Hanover Bay and Point Cunningham smaller but more accessible supplies.

Phillip Parker King was one of the greatest of Australia's early nautical surveyors. The son of NSW Governor, Philip Gidley King, the younger King was born on Norfolk Island in 1791 and died in Sydney in 1856. Much of his work was carried out in a series of voyages along the Kimberley coast. He was also the first Australian-born rear-admiral in the British navy. King's early voyages along the north-west coast (from 1818) were in the 84-ton cutter *Mermaid*; his last voyage to the Kimberley in 1821-1822 was in the 170-ton *Bathurst*.

■ A sturdily built vessel, the British 10-gun brig *Beagle* (on the right in the painting, right) made a significant contribution to exploration of the Kimberley, and the Australian coast generally, between 1838 and 1843. The crew, under the command of Captain John Wickham, filled in the gaps on the chart left by Phillip Parker King. This painting, "Valparaiso 1834", was painted by Conrad Martens.

■ Sir George Grey (below) (1812–1898) had a more distinguished career in his later life than any other early Kimberley explorer. He became Governor of SA, New Zealand (twice), and Cape Colony (later part of South Africa).

This close examination of the coast was not without risk. On more than one occasion the racing tides almost cost King his ship, flinging it towards islands, reefs and rocks. The bay named Disaster stands as a reminder of one close shave. Further to the east, Encounter Cove marks one scene of conflict between King's party and local Aboriginals.

John Clements Wickham and George Grey

Towards the end of 1836, British interest in the north-west of Australia intensified to the degree that the Government funded two further explorations in a single expedition under the over-all control of Captain John Clements Wickham. The groups set sail in the *Beagle* on 5 July 1837. Their instructions were to explore and survey those portions of the Australian coast left uncharted by earlier expeditions. In particular, they were to search with the utmost care for the extensive rivers that King and Dampier believed must empty into the large bays to the west of the Prince Regent River.

While Wickham's party used the *Beagle* to survey the coast, Lieutenant George Grey, whose party was sponsored by the Royal Geographical Society, was to explore the countryside. Landing at the Prince Regent River, he was to follow the coast southwards, towards the Swan River, so that he would inevitably cut across any rivers flowing westward from the interior.

Grey chartered an extra vessel, the *Lynher*, at Cape Town and sailed directly to Hanover Bay and the mouth of the Prince Regent River. Wickham, in the *Beagle*, proceeded via the Swan River Colony (established in 1829). A severe attack of dysentery delayed him by six weeks and, by the time the *Beagle* reached the Kimberley in January 1838, Grey had established a temporary camp at Hanover Bay and was waiting for the *Lynher* to return from Timor with livestock and tropical plants.

Despite King having clashed with the Aboriginal people at Hanover Bay, that place afforded the easiest known access to fresh water on this coast. It also provided anchorage in which the *Lynher* could wait in comparative safety while Grey explored the surrounding countryside. It was at Hanover Bay that Grey introduced many exotic plants and animals – including ponies, sheep, goats, pumpkins, breadfruit, coconuts and cotton – to Australia. These were intended primarily for his own use but also with a view to fostering future colonies in the area.

From time to time, the Aboriginal people engaged the explorers in battle. Grey himself was wounded, which curtailed his exploration and, with other impediments, prevented any attempt at following the coast south to the Swan River.

In the space of three months, Grey's party penetrated inland as far as the headwaters of the Glenelg and Sale rivers. Although unable to find a major river system, Grey was immensely impressed by the land and harbours he saw. He intended to return to the Kimberley with colonists but, when he arrived home, he found he couldn't raise the support necessary to implement his plan.

Wickham's party was more successful than Grey's in discovering rivers. The *Beagle* reached Roebuck Bay in mid-January and surveyed the coast from there to Port George IV before meeting up with Grey in April. Withstanding swarms of voracious mosquitoes, which inspired their naming of Point Torment, sailors braved the powerful tidal rips of King Sound to examine the Fitzroy River.

Squally weather and the sheer power and volume of water surging in and out of the mouth of the Fitzroy made the exploration hazardous. Nevertheless, a gig and a whaleboat pushed 36 km up the river. Although pleased with their find, the sailors noted debris in trees an astonishing 7 m above the water and concluded, correctly, that heavy floods sometimes swept this countryside.

Land exploration

Subsequent British efforts to establish colonies in northern Australia focused on the Northern Territory. It was not until 1853 that the Royal Geographical Society once again persuaded the British Government to look favourably upon the Kimberley region and at the question of rivers flowing from the interior.

Examining the Victoria River in 1855, Augustus Charles Gregory, leader of the North Australian Exploring Expedition, noticed that this river's major tributaries came from the

■ The town of Kimberley in South Africa and the Kimberley region of Australia were both named in honour of John Wodehouse, 1st Earl of Kimberley (1826–1902) (below). A liberal statesman, he was Colonial Secretary at the time both settlements were being established – one on the world centre of diamond mining, the other with great pastoral potential. Unexpectedly, a century later, Australia's Kimberley was found to have enough diamonds to support the world's largest diamond mine.

■ The Ord River (below, lower) was among the elusive fresh water sources that European explorers had long sought.

Plants found in New Holland.

F. 1.

2.

4.   3.

west. He took a small party westward along the northern edge of the desert and cut the course of Sturt Creek. In the summer heat, four men and 11 horses plodded from one waterhole to the next, tracing the creek bed almost 500 km south to Lake Gregory (which was dry at the time). Had they taken a more northerly route into Western Australia, they would probably have found the Ord and solved part of the riddle of the western rivers.

Pastoral expansion in the south and east of Australia began to place huge demands on the continent's grasslands and, by the late 1870s, European exploration of the Kimberley interior was inescapable. The West Australian surveyor, Alexander Forrest, took the opportunity to open the last of the continent's unexplored plains for pastoral use, an enterprise in which he and his associates had more than a passing interest.

Forrest arranged for pastoralists in the Pilbara region (south of the Kimberley) to fit out his party with horses and provisions. He secured funding from the Western Australian Government partially on the strength of the possibility that his party might find gold, an incentive that no doubt added to his sponsors' enthusiasm for the project.

The expedition sailed from Fremantle to the Pilbara in January 1879, then rode from De Grey River station to Eighty Mile Beach. Fresh water was as scarce as mosquitoes were plentiful. The need for supplies of drinking water brought Forrest and his companions into contact with Aboriginals. Initially, the locals were fearful of the intruders but, as the party drew closer to Beagle Bay, a recent history of amicable encounters with outsiders made the local people more approachable.

Persistent efforts to find a way through the King Leopold Ranges cost Forrest dearly in horses and the health of his party. He was finally obliged to abandon this quest and make his way to the Overland Telegraph line in the Northern Territory. In doing so he came across the Margaret and Ord rivers. He estimated the fertile river plains would carry thousands of head of sheep. All told, Forrest claimed to have opened up 25 million acres (10 million ha) of new land for pastoral use.

In the Kimberley, Forrest's party had surprisingly little contact with Aboriginals. He recorded some opposition on their part but none that actually resulted in battle. Aboriginal tolerance of his party may have been enhanced by the unusually good season and by the fact that, in general, these explorers did not seek out or directly interfere with the people living there.

Forrest's exploration was directly responsible for opening up the Kimberley to European settlement and the Western Australian Government was keen to have settlers take up the land. To capitalise on the money available from the Victorian gold rush, it touted for settlers at the Melbourne Exhibition of 1880. This boosted interest in the Kimberley among eastern colonial squatters and some sent livestock across the continent to take part in Australia's last major land grab. Right from the moment Forrest's favourable report became public, it was inevitable that the Kimberley was soon to receive its first permanent European settlers. So began the series of overlanding adventures whose scope still causes amazement.

The MOGULS

COU NTREY

BEN GALA   CHINA   Fokien   Amoy   Formosa I.

The Tropick of Cancer

Surat   Aracam   TONQUIN   Bashee I.

Bombay   Masulipatan   BAY of   Pegu   Bay of Tonquin   Pangasinam   The
Goa   Ladrone
Malabar   BENGALE   SIAM   COCHIN   Mancile   I. Luconia   THE PHILLIPPINE   I. Guam   Islands
Coromandel   Pallacat   Siam   CHINA   Shalel of   Philippine I.
St. George   I. Andeman   Champa   Pearl   PRAGOYA   ISLANDS   I. St. John
Pontucheri   Cambodia   I. Mindora   I. St. John
Porto Novo   Bay of   I. of Paragua Stile   I. Meangis
C. Comorin   Ceylon I.   Siam   Siam   I. Banay   Mindanao   THE SPICE
I. Nicobar   Cudda   Pulo Condor   I. Tidore   I. Cilolo   The Equator
Colombo   Wi   Malacca   Borneo   B. of Chambongo
Achin   MALACCA
I. of Hogs   Bor neo   Celebes   N. Guinea

Maldivas   SUMATRA   Suckindana   Ambon   I. Banda
I. Nassau   Bendarmas   I. Timor   ISLANDS
Indrapore   I. Triste
Bencouli   Java I.   Baly
Streights of Sundy   Bantam   Cumbava
Batavia
THE INDIAN SEA   I. Cocos

NEW HOLLAND

The Tropick of Capricorn

or TERRA AUSTRALIS

INCOGNITA.

300   600   900   1200   1500
English Miles.

A Map of the
EAST INDIES

A map from William Dampier's *A New Voyage Around The World* (1697) (above) and Dampier's drawings of the plants of "New Holland" (opposite). History has proved correct Dampier's judgement that "New Holland is a very large Tract of Land. It is not yet determined whether it is an island or a main Continent; but I am certain that it joins neither to Asia, Africa, nor America".

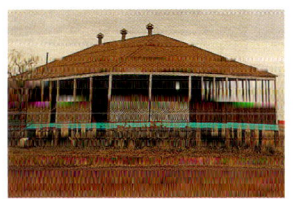

EARLY EUROPEAN SETTLEMENT

The most remarkable feature of European settlement in the Kimberley is that it is so recent: the region was one of the last in Australia to receive European immigrants. Their enduring occupation of the Kimberley didn't begin until 1879 or, in some parts, until the 1920s or even later. This is still within living memory of today's inhabitants. When you talk of European settlement of the Kimberley, therefore, you are discussing the actions of parents and grandparents – recent generations. There are some names that crop up time and again, Emanuel, MacDonald and Durack among them. Because of the thread of common experience, the people from the pioneering families often speak of others dead before the turn of the 20th century as though they had just left the room.

Pastoral industry

The initial steps towards setting up a pastoral industry in the Kimberley were taken long before Alexander Forrest and his party left the first bootprints across the region. Early in 1863, liberal new land laws came into effect in Western Australia and allowed anyone who took stock north of the Murchison River to occupy land there rent-free for the first four years. Those who first decided to take up this offer in the Kimberley focused their attention on the areas and harbours explored by George Grey in 1838. Despite their best endeavours, none of the ventures proved long lasting.

First off the mark were eight Western Australians led by Kenneth Brown. They sailed north in the schooner *Flying Foam* in June 1863, carrying enough stores for four months exploration and 12 months occupation, as well as 7 horses, 25 sheep and 2 dogs. Establishing a base on the Glenelg River, which flows into George Water to the south-west of the Prince Regent River mouth, Brown's party explored the coast and surrounding hinterland. Clashes occurred with Aboriginals and then, having found insufficient grazing land for their needs, the party decided against settlement. In 1864, a government-sponsored expedition, in the aptly named *New Perseverance*, investigated tales of a gold find at Camden Harbour south-east of Camden Sound. The find turned out to be fictitious but the party entered Roebuck Bay and set up a depot near Cape Villaret before returning to Fremantle.

By this time, sheep graziers had taken up land in the Pilbara. In November 1864, the Western Australian-based Roebuck Bay Pastoral and Agricultural Association (Limited) made camp at Cape Villaret.

Vast open spaces (opposite) and long periods without rain were among the challenges facing early settlers in the Kimberley. Patriarch of his extensive and influential family, Michael Patrick Durack (1865–1950) (inset opposite) was a son of "Patsy" Durack, the instigator of the Durack cattle drive from Queensland to the Kimberley and the founder of Argyle Downs station.

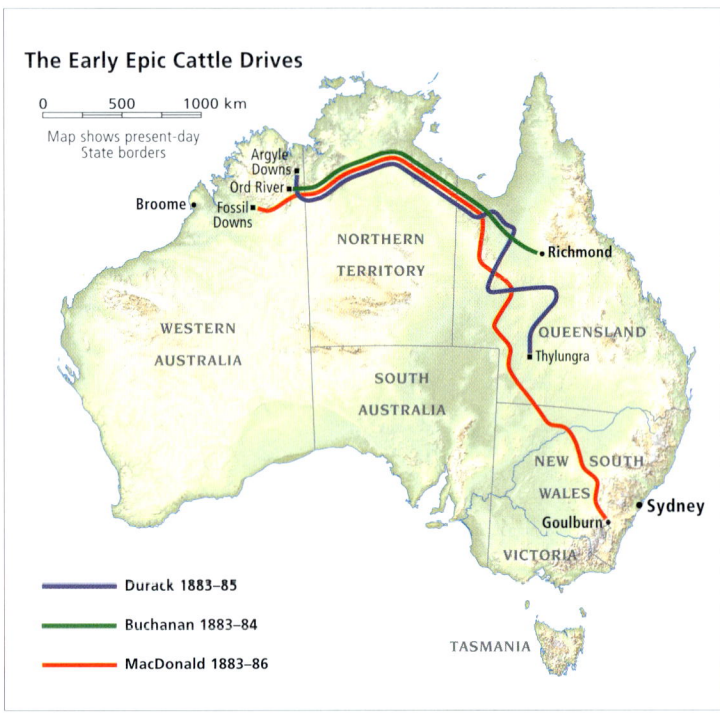

The Early Epic Cattle Drives

0   500   1000 km

Map shows present-day
State borders

Argyle
Downs
Ord River
Broome
Fossil
Downs

NORTHERN

TERRITORY

Richmond

WESTERN

AUSTRALIA

QUEENSLAND

Thylungra

SOUTH

AUSTRALIA

NEW SOUTH

WALES

Goulburn   Sydney

VICTORIA

TASMANIA

Durack 1883–85

Buchanan 1883–84

MacDonald 1883–86

The paths of early epic cattle drives to settle the Kimberley, shown in the map (above), spanned the continent.

The manager, James Harding, with Constable Goldwyer and Police Inspector Panter (colonial police often provided protection for pioneer pastoralists) left to look for grazing land towards Lagrange Bay. They used guns and dogs to keep the indigenous people away from waterholes and, when conflict followed, the explorers were killed. Months later an expedition led by Brown recovered their remains and dispensed savage retribution.

Meanwhile, another sheep-farming settlement had been formed by Victorians at Camden Harbour. The venture struggled to survive and finally succumbed to harsh climatic extremes, poor pasture and Aboriginal resistance. Some of the settlers went home while others tried the more amenable Pilbara. The Roebuck Bay company considered moving to the Fitzroy River region after Alexander McRae rode there from Cape Villaret in May 1866 but that move never eventuated. Instead, sheep farming in the Kimberley was abandoned until Alexander Forrest's exploration and survey of 1879.

Forrest's journey and journals provided the impetus for two groups of Kimberley settlers who had very little in common. Sheep graziers travelled to the west Kimberley by sea from elsewhere in Western Australia, from New South Wales and Victoria. They relied heavily on local Aboriginals as shepherds (until the late 1880s when fenced paddocks came into use). In the east, pastoralists arrived from Queensland and New South Wales, some with the cattle they overlanded. These settlers always favoured open-range grazing that required no fences, a style of management that, on the whole, proved practical until disease control and breeding programs began to require better stock control.

Land distribution

The Western Australian Government printed copies of Forrest's report and used it as a prospectus at its stand at the Melbourne Exhibition in 1880. It then held a ballot for all parties interested in Kimberley land on 1 February 1881. As an attempt to ensure fair land distribution, the ballot was a monumental failure. One cartel of shareholders from the Kimberley Pastoral Company lodged 160 of the 448 applications and secured extensive frontages to the Fitzroy and Meda rivers. Luluigui, Liveringa and Meda stations were the result. Forrest had not been permitted to participate in the ballot because of his official role as a government surveyor but by 1882 he was a member of the Kimberley Pastoral Company. By 1883 he and his associates held most of the prime land in the west Kimberley. Yet William Marmion, the guiding force behind the most powerful of the region's early land-owning concerns, never even visited the Kimberley.

Some sheep graziers had rushed their stock into the Kimberley after Forrest's expedition and before the ballot. These flocks reached the Fitzroy River in March 1881. Some went onto the Murray Squatting Company's Yeeda station on the Fitzroy River; others eventually stocked Balmaningarra station on the Lennard River.

In November 1884, the Emanuel family, which went on to become one of the leading Kimberley families, shipped its first sheep to King Sound. The family diversified into cattle

■ Returning at the end of an all-day camel drive (left), tourists cross Cable Beach near Broome. Camels were introduced to the Kimberley during the gold rush of 1886 to bring supplies from Derby. Strangely, some of Australia's first camels arrived in Hobart in 1840, although most were later introduced into the more suitable dry areas of SA. By 1901 there were about 400 Afghan and Indian cameleers in Australia and one, Adroman Khan, had a string of 25 camels delivering tea, flour and other supplies to Kimberley stations.

■ Dick Smith (below) reflects on the poignant history of Mary Jane Pascoe, who died at Camden Harbour on 4 June 1865, aged 30, soon after giving birth to the settlement's first child. Records suggest the baby died two months later on 11 August 1865; the cause of death was not recorded.

in 1885 and moved to the Fitzroy River the following year to establish Lower Liveringa and, some years later, Noonkanbah and Gogo stations.

The colonial government did not require advance payment of any of the annual rent on the first pastoral leases. In effect, anyone could secure one million acres or more of the Kimberley for no more than an application fee of two shillings and sixpence and then hang on to it in the hope that someone would be prepared to buy the lease before the rent was due. Many parcels of Kimberley land became mere gambling chips held by entrepreneurs who had no interest in stocking their properties. Inevitably, land speculation was rife and this unproductive manipulation greatly slowed pastoral development. In 1883, over 51 million acres (about 21,000 sq. km) of the Kimberley were leased but market forces rationalised that to about 14 million (about 5670 sq. km) by 1887.

Much of the fascination the Kimberley holds for Australians who know its story stems from the astounding cattle-droving feats of the eastern colonial overlanders. Three names stand out: Buchanan, MacDonald and Durack.

■ The gracious foyer of Fossil Downs homestead (right), completed by Maxine and Bill MacDonald just after World War II, represented a new age of permanence in the Kimberley after decades of "making do" and "near enough is good enough for the bush". A waterbag from the original MacDonald cattle drive, the world's longest, takes pride of place on the bloodwood staircase. Nearby, award ribbons for cattle cover one wall.

■ Nat Buchanan (1826-1901) (below) was the first person to overland cattle into the Kimberley (for Osmand and Panton), arriving at what was to be Ord River station in June 1884. He also pioneered the infamous Murranji Track stock route from Newcastle Waters to the Victoria River.

Nat Buchanan

The first of these early pioneers is a legend of Australian pastoral history. Nat "Paraway" Buchanan was born in Ireland in 1826 and died on his farm near Tamworth, NSW in 1901. He was called "Paraway" after the Aboriginal pronunciation of "far away", his invariable answer when asked where he had come from. The first cattle he took to the Kimberley were not his own: he was droving Osmand and Panton's stock from central Queensland to their leasehold, which became Ord River station. Buchanan assumed control of this drive on the Flinders River below Richmond in May 1883 and arrived on the Ord in June 1884.

This pioneer pastoralist, drover and explorer also opened up the Murranji Track in the Northern Territory in 1886 while taking horses from Queensland to Wave Hill station. Immediately after this, he pushed 300 head of Wave Hill cattle through unknown country to form a new station on Sturt Creek and started butchering on the Halls Creek diggings. Parts of his route through the Northern Territory are now followed by the Buchanan Highway.

Fossil Downs

The man behind the establishment of Fossil Downs, a property of just over one million acres (4000 sq. km) near Fitzroy Crossing, never saw the result of his dream. Donald MacDonald's imagination was fired by the potential of this distant new region after he exchanged letters about it with Alexander Forrest. MacDonald's descendants still hold the letters, and Fossil Downs, but MacDonald himself died less than 12 months after his sons established the station.

They left Tuena, near Goulburn, NSW, in March 1883 with 420 head of cattle and 36 draught bullocks. The MacDonalds' herd arrived at Fossil Downs, 5600 km distant, just over three years later. It was the world's longest cattle drive and the bullock wagon that survived the odyssey through to Derby is believed to be the first vehicle to cross the Australian continent. Today, Fossil Downs is owned and managed by Donald MacDonald's great grand-daughter Annette and her husband John Henwood. They had previously managed it for Annette's mother, Mrs Maxine MacDonald, a true Kimberley pioneer who died in 1988.

The Duracks

The story of the Duracks was brilliantly told by Dame Mary Durack in *Kings in Grass Castles* and *Sons in the Saddle*. Several waves of Duracks and their stock left Thylungra station on Cooper Creek and other Queensland cattle stations in June, July and August 1883. More than two years later, at the end of the drive in September 1885, "Long Michael" Durack (as distinct from "Stumpy Michael" Durack who was the first to hold a lease over part of what is now known as the Bungle Bungle Range) created an east Kimberley landmark when he carved his initials on a tree near the Ord River.

The Duracks established Argyle, Dunham River, Ivanhoe and Lissadell stations. In April 1989, Spirit Hill, the only station in the north still owned by a Durack – located just across the Northern Territory border from Ivanhoe station – was sold by Reg and Enid Durack.

The gold rush

As in other parts of Australia where gold was found, a gold rush gave Kimberley development an enormous boost. Indeed, the short-lived rush had an impact out of all proportion to the size of the find. Poor communications from this far corner of the continent ensured that many fortune seekers were just arriving when the majority of disillusioned diggers were pulling out.

On 2 September 1872 the Colony of Western Australia had offered a reward of £5000 to anyone who discovered a workable goldfield within 300 miles (500 km) of any declared port in the colony. That immediately triggered a lot of interest but the first indication that there was gold in the Kimberley was when a geologist with Alexander Forrest's expedition of 1879 suggested that the source of the Fitzroy River might be gold bearing. Soon after, Patrick Ahern and a mate rode in from the Northern Territory to prospect the area. Neither was seen again.

A better-equipped and more fortunate party led by Philip Saunders, a well-known prospector, rode from the Pilbara through the Kimberley to the Northern Territory in 1882. Although their expedition was dogged by illness, they found traces of gold around the upper Ord River. Saunders and others then offered to undertake government-sponsored

■ Descendant of the Durack pioneers and chronicler of Kimberley settlement, Dame Mary Durack Miller (above) is best known for *Kings in Grass Castles* (1959). She wrote or co-authored nine other books and many articles on outback life, and until her death in December 1994, Dame Mary, the widow of the pioneer aviator Horrie Miller, lived in Nedlands, a Perth suburb.

Relics of goldmining days, such as the heavily used and roughly mended utensils displayed below, can still be found in areas that were once the scene of hectic gold rush activity. Modern-day fossickers also enjoy searching for gold on the site of the old fields.

prospecting but the government became directly involved only when it sent Edward Hardman, an Irish geologist, to the Kimberley in 1883. He, too, pinpointed the Ord watershed as the most promising area.

Two well-equipped expeditions that examined pastoral land in 1884 also looked for gold but another two men disappeared in the process. Their loss did not deter others, however, and, after the 1884–1885 wet season, small parties of prospectors headed for the upper Ord River area. Then, on 8 August 1885, Charles Hall and John Slattery announced that they had found 10 ounces (283 grams) of nuggetty gold at Halls Creek on 14 July.

After notifying the Government, they attempted to consolidate their claim on the reward by giving their story to the newspapers. Despite this, they never received the money. The Government argued that neither they nor several other claimants fulfilled a specific condition of the reward offer – that the resulting field must produce a certain amount of gold. They probably came undone because there was a duty on gold finds: undoubtedly, a lot of gold left the region undeclared in prospectors' pockets and saddlebags.

However, finder's fee or not, word soon spread on the "bush telegraph" that there was gold in the Kimberley and other prospectors were soon on their way. "Black Pat" Durack and August Lucanus each set up stores at Cambridge Gulf to capitalise on the expected rush; by October they were selling supplies to small parties of diggers. Some city newspapers cautioned that the isolated field had yet to prove its worth but far more tantalising rumours told of the good prospects there. By early 1886 about 50 prospectors were working the area, supported by mates who brought them supplies from the coast.

As more gold came into Derby from the field, gold fever gripped the tiny township and spread throughout Australia and New Zealand. Speculators who had invested heavily in Kimberley land without return saw potential profits in the rush. The combined efforts of merchants, pastoralists, government spokesmen, land speculators and shipping agents led to a flood of Kimberley news in newspapers around Australia. Voices of caution were drowned in the clamour of the thousands heading for the new El Dorado.

By September 1886, the makeshift camps of more than 2000 prospectors dotted the Halls Creek goldfield. The population was almost entirely male and European; Chinese miners were prohibited and a savage punitive expedition had driven Aboriginals from the main field after they killed a prospector in June.

Most of the prospectors had to carry dirt long distances to water to wash it or otherwise search for gold using the much more uncomfortable and less productive dry-blowing method. Heat, fever and dysentery, combined with frequent food shortages and a roaring trade in grog, took their toll. Moving daily from one gully to the next, the ranks of diggers were swelled by newcomers determined enough to proceed past the many disillusioned heading out. But many new prospectors never made it beyond the ports of Derby and Wyndham after receiving discouraging on-the-spot information. Both there and on the field, the wagons, harnesses and spare horses of those who were leaving sold for a pittance.

Many who were on the point of leaving stayed when prospecting uncovered more finds in the 1886 dry season. None of the finds was substantial. When the rains came in December 1886, there were about 800 persevering prospectors in the Kimberley, many looking beyond Halls Creek to areas like Panton River and Mt Dockrell. Continual rumours of new finds kept the hopeful on the move. Only the finders knew how well they really fared, however; few were prepared to let the Government tax their hard-won finds.

By mid-1887, the European population of the goldfield was around 500; a quarter of what it had been less than 12 months earlier. Prospects looked brighter when heavy reefing machinery was brought in but the field continued to disappoint, never matching the illusion conjured by its promoters. It's estimated that the field produced a total of about 23,000 ounces (roughly 650 kg) of gold by 1896. Eventually, most of the diggers moved on, some blazing the trail for the rush on Australia's richest goldfield, Coolgardie, in September 1892. Coolgardie yielded an impressive 3000 ounces (85 kg) in a single month.

By 1890, only 70 Europeans remained at Halls Creek. In all, the Kimberley may have seen as many as 10,000 arrivals during the gold rush. Of those who stayed, some, like Francis Connor and Denis Doherty, became prominent in Kimberley affairs. It was essentially a storekeeper's rush: the instant infrastructure of police stations and postal services, with piecemeal extension of the telegraph line from Perth, was its legacy to pastoralists who otherwise would have waited years for these services.

■ Badly weathered mud brick walls and fireplaces are all that remain of the post office at Old Halls Creek. Once the centre of a highly mobile gold-rush community of 2000, the place is now a ghost town. For practical reasons the residents voted to move to a new site, 14 km away, in 1948 and, over the next 12 years, they re-established all of the essential services there. Old Halls Creek remains a popular visitor destination and, in 2002, after three years of fundraising, the Kimberley Society and the owner of the post office ruins had a roof constructed to conserve them for the future. The roof mimics the original, giving visitors an impression of how the 1889 building once looked.

OPENING UP THE LAND

For its first 40,000 or more years of settlement, the Kimberley was relatively self-contained. Trade routes had been established within the area and there were links with other parts of the continent and with the fishermen of Asia. However, to the European settlers who arrived in the late 19th century, the Kimberley was not sufficient in itself: it was the "remote north-west". It has taken 100 years and more to overcome this isolation. On the way, several Kimberley developments in road and air transport and telecommunications were also milestones in opening up Australia.

Beginnings of the roadway

The initial surge of development of Kimberley supply routes was aimed at servicing the Halls Creek gold rush of 1886. Camels, bullock and horse drays came from Derby, packhorses (and later, camels) from Wyndham. Later, donkeys and mules supplemented the horses when they proved to be more suitable. Inland mail was originally carried by police (and recipients had to collect it from Halls Creek) before contractors took over and made deliveries en route. In 1889, a six-weekly mail service between Wyndham and Halls Creek was introduced. That was the year after the Adelaide Steamship Company won the contract for a six-weekly mail service between Fremantle and Wyndham.

By 1930, pastoralists from as far inland as Halls Creek were using their own motor trucks and cars to collect their stores from the ports.

In the early 1950s, the northern part of the longest classified road in Australia, the Great Northern Highway from Perth through Meekatharra to Wyndham, was described as having "numerous hazardous creek crossings, marshy sections, patches of heavy sand and rocky outcrops". There was no serviceable road link between Wyndham and Darwin: one was developed later to service the Ord River Scheme. Finally, the opening of the Fitzroy Crossing to Halls Creek tar section in September 1986, the last link in an all-sealed Highway One around Australia, gave the Kimberley a road more suitable for the many cars, road trains and ore carriers using it today.

Telecommunications

The Kimberley, with its vast open spaces, widely separated towns and remote homesteads, has always been a region that welcomes advances in communication systems. The facilities available today only highlight all the more clearly the isolation early settlers had to contend with.

Motionless after the evening's last breeze, the gaunt skeleton of a windmill (opposite) is silhouetted by the setting sun. The simple direct-acting windmill is an Australian innovation: each revolution of the blades produces one stroke of the pump. By the mid-1950s it was estimated that Australia had at least 250,000 water-pumping windmills.

GREAT NORTHERN HIGHWAY
FITZROY CROSSING-HALLS CREEK SECTION
THE LAST LINK IN AN AROUND AUSTRALIA SEALED HIGHWAY

A FEDERALLY FUNDED
NATIONAL HIGHWAY PROJECT

JOINTLY OPENED 21 NOVEMBER 1986 BY

THE HON. GAVAN J. TROY B.BUS., J.P., M.L.A.
STATE MINISTER FOR TRANSPORT

AND

GRAEME CAMPBELL M.H.R.
MEMBER FOR KALGOORLIE

REPRESENTING

THE HON. PETER MORRIS M.H.R.
FEDERAL MINISTER FOR TRANSPORT

■ Lumbering giant of northern Australia, a road train (above) drives through Wyndham carrying cattle to the wharf for export. In the absence of a railway, road trains are the only means of carrying bulk cargoes in the Kimberley. The sealing of a section of road generally doesn't warrant a commemorative plaque (left), but when part of a road near Halls Creek was finished in September 1986, it meant that Australia's Highway One, which runs virtually the perimeter of Australia, was finally sealed for its entire length.

telephone The telegraph line from Roebourne, south of Port Hedland, through Roebuck Bay (Broome) to Derby was completed in April 1889. The "goldfields extension" was completed in October 1889, even as the goldfields were dying. After that line was opened it still couldn't be used much in the early days as it frequently failed due to heat, lightning strikes and wind. Also, the Aboriginal people discovered that broken insulators made excellent spear heads and that guy wires were equally useful. Another substantial disadvantage was that no telegraph operator came to the goldfields until six months after the telegraph line was completed. The Wyndham Telegraph Station wasn't opened until January 1893.

The townships were the first parts of the Kimberley to come into the Australian telephone network but even their connection lagged well behind just about everywhere else in Australia. Individual homesteads far from townships waited even longer. Wyndham and Kununurra were the last towns to join in with a radio-telephone link in 1965. Two years later it was partly replaced by a landline.

Radio Australia's introduction to the age of radio began with the establishment of coastal radio stations, including one in the Kimberley. These were not for entertainment but for ship-to-shore communication. Broome Radio (call sign VIO) started operating in 1913, at least 10 years before regular entertainment radio broadcasts began in Australia and 19 years before the Australian Broadcasting Commission (ABC) was created. Until the 1990s, Radio VIO operated as an information, weather and safety service for shipping reports, and as a radio medical advisory service that linked ships with a shore-based medical officer. However, the bulk of the station's traffic was the exchange of commercial information between vessels and their agents and owners. Communications like these now issue from radio bases in Perth and Darwin.

Although an international submarine cable from Broome to Indonesia ensured that the Kimberley was instrumental in linking Australia to the world from 1889, communications within the region have always been very difficult. Until the 1980s, communication among Kimberley stations and towns and their contact with the rest of Australia and the outside world was haphazard to say the least.

In the late 1920s the pedal radio was developed, allowing remote stations to send radio messages to the Royal Flying Doctor Service (RFDS) bases and, through them, send messages as telegrams via the postal service. Later, when voice transmission became possible, the RFDS could patch radio calls into the telephone network and Kimberley stations had their first direct contact with the rest of Australia.

Until 1986, the chatter of the RFDS radio was a constant background noise in every Kimberley station and outpost. Outside the scheduled broadcast times, "galah sessions" allowed a general exchange of information in which every person with a radio set could participate. There wasn't much privacy but every property felt in touch with others, even when the nearest was many kilometres away.

■ In 1987, Michael Cusack and his wife Susan spent a year at Kunmunya as AUSTRALIAN GEOGRAPHIC's first "Wilderness Couple". Here Michael makes a call from the telephone at Pantijan station, linked to the world by microwave. In keeping with rapid advances in telecommunication, the network of microwave towers has been replaced by optic fibre cable and digital technology. Faxes, mobile phones and the world wide web are now as much a part of life in the Kimberley as they are in the distant cities.

A Telstra microwave tower (above) between Broome and Beagle Bay adds an alien element to the landscape. Decommissioned since this photograph was taken, the tower was a link in what was once the longest solar-powered telecommunication system in the world, drawing the Kimberley into the wider Australian community and no longer reliant solely on sporadic mail deliveries and the Royal Flying Doctor Service radio. The ongoing installation by Telstra of optic fibre cable and Digital Mobile Base Stations has ensured the Kimberley will benefit from the revolution in electronic communications.

However, in November 1982 the national telephone system was extended by microwave to Broome and Derby. The Kimberley Microwave System was further extended to Wyndham and Kununurra in September 1983. The final link in the circuit, through to Katherine, NT was added in 1987. Once the longest solar-powered microwave system in the world, by 1998 it was already obsolete, replaced by optic fibre cable and Digital Mobile Base Stations. By the end of the 20th century, optic fibre had reached El Questro Wilderness Park and Wyndham and Kalumburu were linked by digital radio. Although some miss the close community spirit that was engendered by the open radio conversations, there is no denying the "communications revolution" brings enormous benefits to the once remote Kimberley.

Television Television first came to the Kimberley in 1985 through ABC broadcasts. At first it was only available to the towns but the launch of Aussat made ABC television accessible to anyone with a satellite receiver. The Golden West Network was introduced to Kununurra, Wyndham, Halls Creek, Broome and Derby in 1986 and to Fitzroy Crossing in 1988.

School of the Air

It looks just like any small country school – brightly coloured children's paintings cover the walls, books and posters abound. However, apart from the infrequent visitor in town for a day or two, few of this school's 70 students see it more than once or twice a year.

This is the Kimberley School of the Air (SOTA), based in Derby, and its "classroom" spreads out over the entire Kimberley. It gives lessons to children from pre-primary school age through to Year 7 on stations from Nicholson in the east, Kandiwal Aboriginal Community in the north and Kalyeeda in the south. On weekdays, each class has an on-air time of between 30 and 40 minutes. Classes themselves include up to six students so that each pupil can be given enough individual attention.

The school owes its existence to the size of Western Australia - the "classroom" is larger than many European countries - and is a triumph of ingenuity over daunting logistics. It works through the Flying Doctor radio and has two frequencies dedicated to the school. Now housed in its own purpose-designed building at Derby District High School, the school is part of the Education Department of Western Australia and, as in other schools, education is free. Classroom materials (everything from computers and printers, to library books, sports equipment, maths equipment and CD-ROM-based software) are provided by SOTA.

For a week each year, the students and their "home tutors" (the mothers in most cases) meet the teachers at a school camp in Derby. Although it is a good chance for the children to see what the other kids behind the voices in the class look like, this is mainly a chance for the home tutors to be given assistance and guidance by the teachers. Once a year, all the senior students (who are within a few years of going to boarding school) spend two weeks in Perth with other students and teachers from the other five SOTAs in Western Australia. Direct personal contact is also given by teachers who visit their remote students at least three times each year - visits that are warmly anticipated by all involved. But for most of the year school is a microphone and the teacher is a loudspeaker and a computer screen. Even so, close relationships exist between teachers and their distant charges.

The uniqueness of SOTA will soon take on a new dimension. The Flying Doctor radio system is to be phased out and replaced by a satellite based computer system including the latest in shared software applications and 24 hour Internet access. While the Kimberley is and always will be a big region, the world outside will be just that little bit closer to home - which is what SOTA is all about.

Aviation

The sparsely settled Kimberley has always been receptive to advances in aviation. And as the first sea navigators made landfalls in the Kimberley and the Northern Territory because these were the closest points to Asia, early aviators' first view of Australia was frequently the Kimberley coast. Indeed, Derby remains the site of a major navigation aid for commercial aircraft en route from Singapore to Sydney and Melbourne.

The first airmail service in Australia commenced between Geraldton and Derby in 1921. This was the same year that the company, Western Australian Airways Ltd, owned by Norman Brearley, employed Charles Kingsford Smith as one of its pilots. "Smithy", who had served as a fighter pilot over the Western Front, was later involved in great controversy after a Kimberley flight.

The first crossing of the Pacific, the first non-stop flight across Australia and the first trans-Tasman flight (and return) had all made Kingsford Smith and co-pilot Charles Ulm national celebrities. Their aircraft, the *Southern Cross*, was one of the best known and most loved objects in Australia. So the eyes of the nation were upon them in March 1929 when they took off to fly non-stop from Richmond, NSW, to Wyndham and then on to England. After encountering a storm and running low on fuel, the *Southern Cross* landed on the mudflats at the mouth of the Glenelg River south of Camden Sound. A massive search was launched and the aviators were found 12 days later. They had survived on a diet of mud snails, the small supply of food in the aircraft and weak coffee laced with brandy, a mixture they jokingly named "Coffee Royal". Unfortunately, two old flying friends of Smithy's had died during the search and a rumour spread that the forced landing was a publicity stunt gone wrong. The Prime Minister ordered an inquiry. Although this completely cleared Smith and Ulm, rumours about the "Coffee Royal" affair lingered for years after. Kingsford Smith successfully completed the flight to London in June the same year in 12 days and 18 hours.

In 1931, the speed record for a flight from Australia to England was broken twice by aircraft leaving from Wyndham. Both were de Havilland Moths. The first such occasion was when C.W.A. Scott took 10 days, 23 hours, a time soon eclipsed by Jimmy Mollison's flight time of 8 days, 21 hours and 25 minutes. Then, in 1933, Kingsford Smith landed in Wyndham only 7 days, 4 hours and 38 minutes after leaving England.

Now housed in its own quarters at Derby District High School, the Kimberley School of the Air brings students from a vast area, many living on stations hundreds of kilometres from neighbours, into an on-air "classroom". Occasional meetings at the school camps are the students' only contact with their teachers and classmates.

A maze of sandbanks, mudflats and mangroves (above) near the Glenelg River was the scene of one of the most harrowing events in the lives of pioneer aviators Charles Kingsford Smith and Charles Ulm. A forced landing (left) left them stranded near here for two weeks in 1929 but both were rescued unhurt. The real tragedy was that two of the search pilots died. Rumours spread that Smithy's "disappearance" was a publicity stunt. The four-man crew was later completely exonerated in a public inquiry into the incident.

Commercial Aviation Development of commercial aviation in the north west of Western Australia became very much the domain of MacRobertson Miller Aviation (MMA), founded in 1927 by former fighter pilot Horrie Miller with money supplied by chocolate magnate Sir Macpherson Robertson. Its break came when it won the government contract to fly mail between Perth and Daly Waters, NT. In 1949, the company pioneered the air transport of chilled beef from Glenroy station to Wyndham meatworks. MMA was bought by Ansett Airlines in 1969, later becoming Ansett WA and then Ansett Australia. Qantas and Virgin Blue both now provide a regular commercial service to the Kimberley and two other airlines, Skipper Aviation and Airnorth, operate regional services. Horrie Miller, who was married to the late Dame Mary Durack Miller (her books are published under her maiden name), died in 1980 and there is a monument to him in Weld Street, Broome.

Aviation continues to play a vital role in the Kimberley. Every station and community has an airstrip and the major regional airports are host to a mixture of the commercial airlines' aircraft, charter operators (fixed-wing and helicopter), the Royal Flying Doctor Service, an assortment of mining and pastoral planes and a regular stream of aircraft "just passing through". Although these aircraft are closely monitored by air traffic control in Derby and Kununurra, there's still an element of adventure about flying in the Kimberley – a lot of areas are still uninhabited and there's plenty of "tiger country" where there is nowhere at all safe to land.

■ Initiated as an innovative alternative to long cattle drives along bad tracks, the Air Beef abattoirs were built at Glenroy station (above) in the east Kimberley in 1949. Here, cattle were slaughtered and chilled before being flown to Wyndham for freezing and export to the UK. In 1965, the year after the Beef Road opened, the abattoirs closed. They burnt down the following year. Since the closure of the Broome meatworks in 1994, live export of cattle through the ports at Broome and Wyndham makes up the bulk of cattle turnoff.

■ Landing on Lake Kununurra (left), this Cessna 206 float plane is one of many operating in the Kimberley. Great expanses of the region have no airfields and float planes or helicopters are often the only easy means of access.

ROYAL FLYING DOCTOR SERVICE

In most homesteads in the Kimberley, as elsewhere in remote parts of Australia, the ubiquitous Royal Flying Doctor Service of Australia Medical Chest is to be found.

In the chest there is a wide range of medicines, in most cases supplied free, each with the name and a number clearly displayed. There is also a simple chart and notes to help the layperson explain pain and symptoms for diagnosis over the radio. For many people on isolated stations where medical help may be hours away, even by aircraft, self-treatment that goes a long way beyond first aid may be required,

The great advantage of these standardised medical chests is that they enable doctors to administer treatment by remote control. Even someone who is medically illiterate can dish out two tablets of number 62 (from tray B) or smear on some 139 (from tray A) as instructed by the doctor.

The real genius of the Royal Flying Doctor Service is the utilisation of technology to spread a "mantle of safety" over the vastness of remote Australia. That phrase was coined by the Reverend John Flynn, of the Australian Inland Mission, whose Flying Doctor Service started in May 1928 when a plane flew from Cloncurry in Queensland to a small bush hospital. However, the technological development that enabled the service to become viable came a few years later when the pedal radio was invented by Alfred Traeger, an Adelaide electrician. This made it possible for just one person to operate a self-contained morse transmitter with a range of almost 500 km. For the first time, people on remote stations could be in instant contact with a doctor.

In the 1930s the Australian Inland Mission handed the flying doctor operation over to a non-denominational honorary body, the Royal Flying Doctor Service, which has sections in several States. The Victorian section, the first to be established (in 1934), doesn't have any "outback" in its own State so it accepted responsibility for the most remote part of Australia: the Kimberley. Now all of Western Australia is covered by a single RFDS, covering the largest area in Australia.

In the Kimberley, there is a Royal Flying Doctor base at Derby and the hangar at Derby airport houses a range of aircraft to suit most remote airstrips.

If the town's hospital can't deal with the case, the patient will normally be flown to a hospital in Perth or Darwin.

Today, most of the medicinal aviation is preventive, not surgical, and takes the form of clinics conducted in remote Aboriginal communities. These are attended by a sister and one or two doctors who see about 600 patients a month. Even in emergencies, the aircraft are used as aerial ambulances not surgeries. Very rarely are surgical operations done on the site.

Until 1987 there were about 100 outback stations tuned into the RFDS radio network, which provided both a social link and an emergency service. However, the introduction of the microwave telephone changed this system. By the end of 1988, nearly all Kimberley stations had microwave telephones and the RFDS radio link was mainly used as a backup if the telephone was down or in conjunction with mobile radios carried by travellers or exploration parties. And now the microwave telephone is itself obsolete, the microwave transmission towers replaced by optic fibre cable and a network of Digital Mobile Base Stations.

Patients don't pay to use the RFDS. Commonwealth and State Governments meet approximately 80 per cent of the annual operating costs, and donations, bequests and fundraising in both Victoria and Western Australia provide for aircraft, medical equipment and other infrastructure costs as well as the balance of running costs.

The Flying Doctor has played a vital part in opening up the Kimberley by providing much-needed security to families whose nearest neighbours may be 100 km or more away. And, as tourist numbers in the Kimberley region increase, the RFDS becomes involved in helping visitors too.

There are 140 airstrips in the Kimberley but only six are sealed and many of the others become unusable after heavy rain. If a station owner cannot guarantee that the strip offers reliable landing (driving along it at 60–80 km/h without skidding is considered a good test), there is still the chance that one of the Kimberley's few helicopters can be called upon. To the city dweller, the RFDS is a clever response to the problems posed by the distances in remote Australia. In the outback, it's a much-appreciated lifeline.

Working into the night the Royal Flying Doctor Service base in Derby prepares for an early morning flight to ensure a patient will be in Perth for what promises to be a difficult birth. From Derby the RFDS casts its "mantle of safety" over the whole Kimberley region.

PRIMARY INDUSTRY

"He's a Kimberley son" is perhaps the highest compliment a man can receive in this corner of Australia. There is an automatic implication that here is someone who was born in the area and has grown up with an intimate knowledge of this harsh and unforgiving country. But more than that, in this land of makeshift buildings and drifting lifestyles, it singles out someone whose family has made a commitment to the Kimberley. A Kimberley son (there is no equivalent expression for daughters) can be expected to have an understanding of a part of Australia that is as unique as the individuals who live there. Like their pioneering forebears, those now living in the Kimberley are still very close to the land and their lives are still governed by the seasons.

Cattle industry

An important part of the cultural fabric of Australia is the part played in its development by the Kimberley cattle kings (so well depicted by the late Dame Mary Durack in *Kings in Grass Castles* and *Sons in the Saddle*). Most of the Kimberley is still closely connected with the cattle industry and although the cattle population has declined, it still represents about 30 per cent of Western Australia's herd, though this figure fluctuates.

Of the Kimberley's 421,000 sq. km, the pastoral industry utilises almost 230,000 sq. km, but despite the impressively large figures, less than 10 per cent of this land can be regarded as high quality pasture,

particularly in the late dry season when there is a lack of feed. Variations in market price also make a crucial difference because of the high fixed costs of transport to distant markets and the vagaries of climate. "Either the beef prices are good, or my cattle are," is the universal complaint of the landholder.

Many Kimberley pastoralists have found the uncertain nature of the industry unbearable and have sold up and moved out, with a trend towards ever-larger properties being concentrated in fewer hands. This is partly due to economies of scale: it has been estimated that a Kimberley cattle station needs a minimum herd of 12,000 head to survive. Even so, most of the properties changing hands greatly exceed these marginal requirements. In 1963 there were 342 pastoral leases in the Kimberley; by 2001 the same amount of land was held under 111 leases, giving the average station an area of about 2072 sq. km.

During the years between 1978 and 1983, when beef prices were low, more than half the Kimberley pastoral leases changed hands and the

Goaded along the race between road train and ship, a Shorthorn (opposite) is on its way from Wyndham's dock to Sabah, Malaysia. Live-cattle exports to Asia are not new to the Kimberley: cattle were being shipped from Derby to Singapore in 1887. Increasingly, the cattle on Kimberely stations today are Zebu, prized for their ability to cope with heat and for their resistance to ticks.

■ Rising above the encroaching vegetation, a tinplate cross (below) marks the grave of pioneer stockman David Suttie. Unlike that of most of his peers, Suttie's memory lives on – he was Dan, the head stockman in Mrs Aeneas Gunn's 1908 classic *We of the Never Never*, in which she documents one year of her life on Elsey station near Katherine in the NT. In 1941, others who featured in the book were brought back and reburied at Elsey station. David Suttie remains where he died in 1912 – at his camp alongside the old Wyndham Road near Black Rock Falls.

■ A stockmen's camp at Mount House station (opposite) is the base used by station workers for several months each year. Cattle are moved, sometimes long distances, to take advantage of the best-available pasture and the stockmen who work with them must be able to cope with a physically strenuous life. Long days in the saddle (opposite, inset) are routine for those in the pastoral industry, particularly on the vast cattle stations of the Kimberley.

total herd size shrank by one-quarter. Nevertheless, the Kimberley continues to carry about 30 per cent of all the cattle in Western Australia, earning about $54 million in 1998-1999.

Traditionally, Kimberley cattle stations had few fences: the cost of building them was regarded as prohibitive and unnecessary. (An oft-repeated Kimberley joke is that the only time you can be sure you're eating your own beef is when you're at a barbecue at your neighbour's place.) The result was a cattle industry much less developed than equivalent operations in the Northern Territory or Queensland.

This, however, has changed, largely because of the greater control required under the brucellosis and tuberculosis eradication program. In a hard-hitting address in the Kimberley in 1986, Mr Brockman of the Pastoralists and Graziers Association of Western Australia declared: "Open-range management is a thing of the past unless you are content to become and remain a peasant farmer."

The reduction in the herd size has had its impact on Kimberley towns, too. Wyndham's large meatworks was opened in 1919 and was the largest single employer in tropical Australia after the Queensland sugar industry. A decline in the number of cattle available for slaughter and industrial disputes led to the meatworks closing at the end of 1985. This was a heavy blow to the town and a large proportion of the population had to move elsewhere. Derby's small abattoir had closed in 1979 and Broome's 15 years later.

Burly Kurt Hammer (below) uses a jeep to herd cattle into the yards for checking prior to shipment. The export of Kimberley cattle is still a thriving business, although additional markets had to be found to compensate for reduced demand from Asian countries during the 1990s. The invaluable road train, a common sight on Kimberley roads, is loaded (right) with cattle for transhipment to the wharf.

Kimberley cattle have traditionally been beef Shorthorns producing predominantly "hamburger beef" for the US market. However, the need for better herd management and destocking to eradicate disease, more fencing and a reduction in pest animals, such as donkeys, have allowed diversification. The market, too, has changed. Historically the Kimberley cattle industry has been disadvantaged by its remoteness from Australia's main population centres, but it is well placed to take advantage of markets in South-East Asia, particularly Indonesia, Malaysia, Brunei and the Philippines. These markets prefer live, young Zebu *(Bos indicus)* cattle or breeds based on it. As these breeds also cope better with heat and are more tick resistant they now comprise virtually all cattle in the Kimberley.

In 1985, the last year that the Wyndham meatworks operated, 45,000 Kimberley and 21,000 Northern Territory cattle were slaughtered at the Broome and Wyndham works. A further 44,000 were sent south for slaughter or sale, 23,000 were moved interstate (mainly for store or sale) and 5500 were shipped to Malaysia. That's a total Kimberley "turn off" of 117,500 cattle. In 2000–2001, 160,846 Kimberley cattle were "turned off", the great majority of these shipped live from the ports of Wyndham, Broome and Darwin.

In the 1990s, the Kimberley cattle industry faced the challenge posed by the economic downturn in Asia and the dramatic decline in exports to this region were largely offset by the development of exports to North Africa and the Middle East. It is a more sophisticated

industry today, with an increasing emphasis on quality over quantity. There is little doubt that the industry that was the backbone of the Kimberley for its first century of European settlement will survive the next 100 years through a balance of conservation and exploitation of the land resources on which it depends. It is worth noting, however, that all Western Australian pastoral leases are due to expire in 2015.

The Ord River Irrigation Area

It began as a dream and developed into a nightmare. Incredible perseverance, however, saw the original Ord River Project eventually become profitable. Now there are plans to expand it and even to set up a similar project in the West Kimberley.

The principle behind the Ord River Project was simple: 75,000 ha of rich clay soil needed only a year-round supply of water to become far more productive than it was as cattle pasture. The Ord River carries a huge volume of water from the Durack Range to the Cambridge Gulf, but nearly all the flow occurs during the wet season. The obvious solution was a dam to ensure a regular water supply to the river flats downstream.

Kimberley Durack of Argyle Downs station started cropping experiments on the Behn River in 1937, and a State Government experimental farm was established on the Ord in 1942. Following successful production of cotton, sorghum and maize, the Kimberley Research Station was established as a joint Federal–State project on the Ivanhoe Plain in 1945.

Results from the research station over the following years showed that sugarcane, rice, cotton, safflower and linseed grew well under irrigation. So, in 1958, more than 20 years after Kimberley Durack had made the first attempts, the Ord River Project was born. The first stage (the diversion dam, irrigation system and Kununurra township) was completed in 1963 at a cost of $20 million. The Kununurra Diversion Dam raised the river level, enabling the Ivanhoe Plain to be irrigated without the need for pumping. Three years later, there were 31 farms under irrigation.

The Ord River Dam, which impounds Lake Argyle, was completed in June 1972 at a cost of $22 million. One of the oldest homesteads in the area, Argyle Downs, established by the Durack family, would have been submerged when the lake filled, so it was moved to its present position and became a museum. Restrained by a dam wall 99 m high and 335 m long, Lake Argyle has a normal capacity of over 10.7 million cubic metres (18 times the volume of Sydney Harbour) and a surface area of 980 sq. km. In times of flood, the dam can hold nearly 35,000 million cubic metres and extends over an area of more than 2000 sq. km.

To prevent the lake filling with the approximately 50,000 tonnes of silt flowing into it each wet season, the Western Australian Government, in 1967, resumed and replanted the leases of several overgrazed cattle properties in the catchment area, including the area around the Bungle Bungle Range.

Although over 60 different crops have been tried under Ord irrigation since 1945, much of the early commercial cropping concentrated on cotton. However, attack by a caterpillar

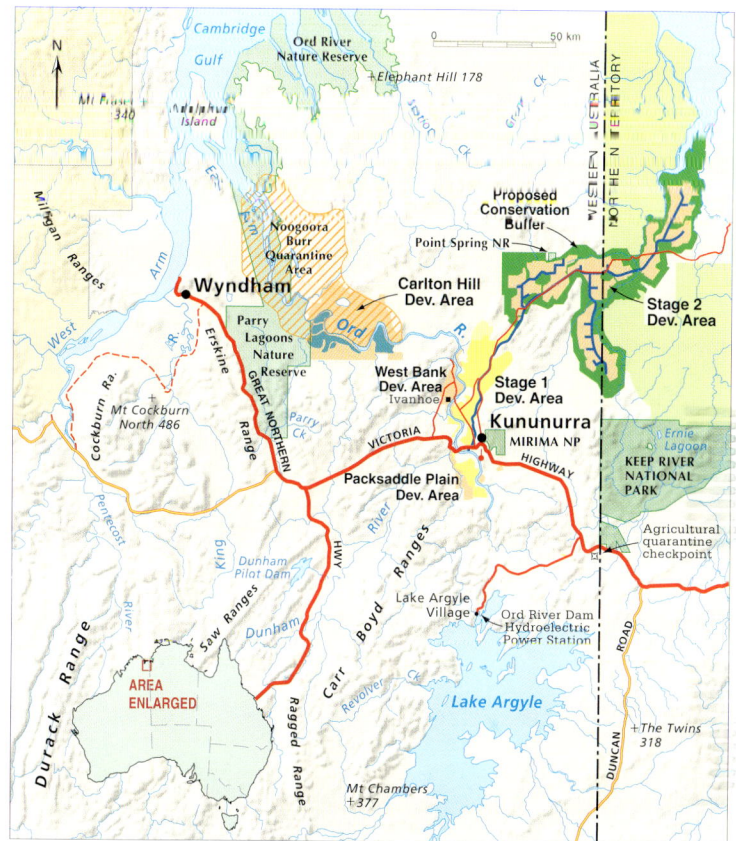

With large areas of suitable country remaining untapped, the map above shows that the original Ord River Project, now the Ord River Irrigation Area (ORIA), still has great scope for development.

Rising 68 m above the original river level, the wall of the Ord River Dam created Lake Argyle, one of the largest artificial lakes in the Southern Hemisphere. Excessive rainfall in the wet season necessitated building the dam over two dry seasons. The half-built dam wall was covered by large rocks and steel mesh which, in February 1971, resisted severe floods up to 30 m deep. The dam was finished later that year.

that proved to be chemical-resistant and the removal of government subsidies killed off this industry in 1974 (today it is back and earns over $1 million per year). Also in 1974 the CSIRO took control of the Kimberley Research Station and the Western Australian Department of Agriculture established its own research facility nearby.

When cotton failed, rice seemed a good alternative. Although grown experimentally in the Kimberley since 1947, rice had not been commercially viable at first because a new variety was required to cope with the Kimberley climate and a zinc deficiency in the soil had to be overcome. This was achieved in the 1970s. However, as had happened with cotton, nature and economics conspired against the new crop. Birds, particularly magpie geese, flocked in for the feast offered by the rice crops during the lean dry season. This depredation, combined with a weak market for rice, resulted in 1983 being the last year of large-scale commercial rice growing.

In 1987, the CSIRO's direct involvement the Ord ended. About the same time, the government stopped handing out subsidies and each crop had to pay its own way. That was the turning point for what is now a very profitable enterprise. In 1986, the development rejoiced in annual profits of $10 million; by 1999-2000 that had risen to $67.5 million. Because the Kimberley is so far from its markets (Perth is 3200 km and Brisbane more than 3500 km away),

■ Handfuls of borlotti beans (left) fill a bag at a roadside vegetable stand outside Kununurra. The variegated borlotti bean is a dried culinary variety grown in the Ord River Irrigation Area (ORIA). Unfortunately, it loses its attractive bands of colour during cooking.

■ Plump mangoes (above) await the fruit pickers on one of the ORIA's many successful horticultural properties. The opportunity to supply "out-of-season" fruit to distant markets helps such ventures thrive.

it needs crops with high returns, such as chickpeas. Kimberley crops also fill a niche in out of season markets in 1999. 3000 bananas, mangoes, watermelons and rockmelons accounted for almost half the value of Ord produce. Overall, it's clear that a wide range of crops is better than a few major crops because that doesn't give pests the same foothold.

One development has taken the Ord riverlands full circle: irrigated pastures are now providing feed for cattle-fattening prior to shipment. This is proving to be very profitable and once again the banks of the Ord River are producing fodder for cattle. There is also a dairy to supply the local market.

Since the late 1990s sugar has come to be one of the most profitable crops in what is now known as the Ord River Irrigation Area (ORIA). Australia's first new sugar mill in nearly 70 years was producing 36,000 tonnes of raw sugar in 2001. That was down considerably over the previous four years, largely as a response to a fall in world sugar prices but it is expected that sugar will continue to be a profitable crop.

Even so, with only 11,000 ha of a potential 70,000 ha being cultivated in the ORIA in 1999–2000, a lot of development is still to come. However, with profits rising almost every year since 1981, the development is certainly paying its way, some 40 years after Kununurra was born to service it.

Converging towards infinity, rows of young soybeans (above) fill a field in the ORIA. These are some of the first grown successfully during the dry season. However, only small quantities of soybeans are now grown – and only during the wet season. Soybean oil is primarily used in food. It also has many other uses in products as diverse as paint, disinfectant, ink and soap.

Barry Lerch – pictured with wife Deanne and their baby Zoe (left) – says that the Ord is one of the few places left in Australia where young farmers can "get in and have a go". He hopes that the area stays in the hands of small farmers rather than be monopolised by large corporations. Growing a diversity of crops rather than just a few helps minimise pests and disease. Sunflower is among the Ord's top money earners.

A field of sugarcane burns with dramatic effect (opposite) against the night sky. The routine burn-off of a cane field prior to harvesting clears weeds and flushes out reptiles and rodents before the harvesters move in.

■ Cockatoo Island (below) has remakably pure iron deposits but they were first used as ballast by pearling luggers. The first mineral lease here in Yampi Sound was issued in 1918 but it was not until 1936 that a survey crew moved into a rudimentary base on the island. The mine facilities were constructed by BHP towards the end of World War II and the first load of ore sailed from the island in 1951.

■ The Argyle Diamond Mine (opposite) cuts deeply into the southern end of the Ragged Range. Twenty million tonnes of rock had to be shifted to expose the 45 ha lamproite diamond-bearing pipe. Ore from the open-cut mine is dumped into the crushing plant on the bill then carried by conveyor belt to the main plant (beside the circular tanks used for water recovery) where it is crushed and separated. A concentrated, diamond-laden mixture goes into the high-security red-roofed building where the diamonds fluoresce under X-rays, activating air valves that blast them to one side.

Mining

Every fortnight a group of workers flies from Perth to the Argyle Diamond Mine. It's an indication of the size and general inaccessibility of the Kimberley that mining companies here use aircraft the way mines in other areas use buses. From the discovery of gold at Halls Creek in 1885 to today's Argyle diamonds, mining has always been an important Kimberley industry. Although mining now accounts for almost half of the region's gross product, the potential mineral wealth is still regarded as under-explored.

Over the past 50 years, much of the mineral interest centred on the iron ore deposits of Yampi Sound, 130 km north of Derby. This part of the Kimberley coast is a mass of islands and bays, long isthmuses and narrow channels where the land falls away to the outcrops of the Buccaneer Archipelago. It's a place of rugged beauty, high rainfall and tidal rips – and what was one of the world's richest bodies of iron ore.

The first Yampi ore was mined at Cockatoo Island in 1951 and that mine had yielded 31 million tonnes of ore when it closed in 1986. It reopened in 1995 with a new beneficiation plant and in the first year produced 700,000 tonnes of iron concentrates for shipment to China. Between 2002 and 2005 it is projected to produce $115 million in iron ore. Nearby Koolan Island loaded its first shipment in 1965. From then till its closure in 1994 it provided 50 million tonnes of high-grade ore for Japanese and Australian steelmakers.

East of Fitzroy Crossing, Pillara Mine and the smaller Kapok Mine are highly efficient underground operations which process 2.9 million tonnes per year of the Lennard Shelf lead-zinc ore body. The ore is partly processed at Pillara and is then trucked to Derby for export. The majority of the mines' 150 employees work on a rotating basis, commuting from Perth, Broome and Derby by air and by road from Fitzroy Crossing and Kununurra. Western Metals Ltd expects that lead-zinc deposits at these existing and future mines will keep the milling operation running for many more years.

Over 200 exploratory oilwells have pierced the Canning Basin so far but only four small fields, about 100 km south-east of Derby, are producing. The oil from these (Blina, Sundown, Lloyd and West Terrace) is piped from Blina to the highway and then trucked to Broome for shipping to the Kwinana refinery south of Fremantle. Production is relatively small and in 1999/2000 produced just $1.4 million of crude oil.

The Kimberley seems to hold the promise of future mineral riches. There is natural gas at Wagon Creek north of Kununurra, and significant resources of oil in the Browse and Bonaparte basins. Also, presently there are uneconomic deposits of 10 million tonnes of lead-zinc ore at Sorby Hills, 35 km north-east of Kununurra and another large underground deposit containing silver and other metals at Koongie Park near Halls Creek. There are also deposits of nickel at Sally Malay Bore, 185 km south-west of Kununurra, that may one day prove economically viable. A 10,000-tonne uranium deposit has been located on Defence Department land at Oobagooma on the Yampi Peninsula and a billion-tonne salt dome identified at Frome Rocks, 130 km south of Derby.

Reserves of bauxite have been discovered in the environmentally sensitive region of the Mitchell Plateau. They may be mined at some time in the future if economic conditions are favourable and if the environmental and social requirements of the day can be met. One proposal includes a smelting operation, fuelled by North West Shelf gas, with a fly-in-fly-out staff and a new port.

Argyle diamonds

The output of the Argyle Diamond Mine makes up almost 80 per cent of the total value of the Kimberley mining and petroleum industries.

With the quite recent discovery of diamonds near Lake Argyle, the Australian Kimberley found it had much more in common with its South African namesake than just boab (or baobab) trees. It is a strange coincidence that the Earl of Kimberley's name was given to two places that have some of the richest diamond fields in the world.

Yielding one gram of diamonds for every tonne of rock, the primary stockpile (top) has been through initial crushing but will be further reduced to pieces no larger than 6 mm.

Flanked by telephones, panel operators (above) in the control room oversee the entire Argyle plant, which is controlled by computers using software developed in Australia.

Australia's first diamonds were found in northern New South Wales and central Victoria in the latter half of last century. Some have also been discovered in South Australia, north-west Tasmania and southern Queensland but none of the deposits has been commercially viable. A few stones had been found in parts of Western Australia prior to 1979 but, again, nothing worth mining.

On 28 August 1979 the Perth laboratory of a prospecting venture found two diamonds in a sample from Smoke Creek in the Kimberley. The next day's sample had four stones in it, the following day's take had five. Following these traces, geologists walked onto and recognised the main diamond-bearing pipe on 2 October 1979. It is in a valley at the southern end of the Ragged Range, 35 km upstream from Lake Argyle.

The resulting Argyle Diamond Mine is now fully owned by Rio Tinto. The mine, one of the most modern in the world, cost $465 million to build. Using X-ray recovery techniques and fully computerised operation, this open-pit mine will recover 30 million carats (about 5 tonnes) of diamonds per year until 2007. That makes it the most productive diamond mine in the world, annually producing about 35 per cent of the world's diamonds. Up to 2003 the mine had produced over 600 million carats of diamonds. However, only 5 per cent of the diamonds mined are of gem quality. A further 70 per cent are in a category known as "near gem quality" and the remaining 25 per cent are industrial diamonds.

The diamonds are sent to Perth for sorting. Since 1996 Argyle has sold all its own diamonds independently, either on the open market through its office in Antwerp in Belgium or, for the most valuable gems, by tender. Argyle diamonds are unique. They are harder than those found elsewhere and a large proportion are bronze or yellow. The mine is also the world's only source of the rare and particularly valuable pink diamonds that regularly fetch over $150,000 per carat. One pink diamond was valued at $1 million per carat.

Although the mine is in a quite remote area, Argyle prides itself on its good relationship with neighbouring Aboriginal communities; a relationship that has developed beyond work opportunities to joint ventures and training programs.

The only public access to the mine is on one of several one-day flying tours from Kununurra. As one would expect, security is very tight in and around the mine area; there are also random body-searches on people leaving. A new feature for visitors is a "Diamond Gallery" that showcases the history of the mine and a range of diamonds and jewellery.

The mine works continually with two 12-hour shifts per day. However, conditions at the mine, which is more than 100 km from any town, are far from unpleasant. The company's mining village features dining rooms, bars, a sail-shaded swimming pool, tennis courts and motel-style rooms for each worker. Most of the 800 mine staff commute from Perth by air, staying at the mine for a work period of 6 to 14 days before heading back for time off.

It was once thought that Argyle would be reaching the end of its working life about now. But there are plans for the mine to go underground in 2005 and then it is projected to continue operating until 2020.

Pearling

The traditional image of pearling is of a rough-and-ready trade, pursued by gamblers, a trade in which every oyster holds the promise of a fortune, and death by misadventure awaits the careless. By comparison with this romantic image, pearling today is a very scientific profession, in which the oysters of the pearl farms are treated as carefully as pedigreed stock on a cattle station. But no matter how much the industry has changed since the days of the early pearlers, Broome is still one of the world's most important pearl centres. It has been since the 1890s.

Modern techniques of growing cultured pearls were developed in Japan, where early this century Kokichi Mikimoto was the leading pioneer. These techniques were introduced by the CSIRO to the Torres Strait pearl trade in 1949. The move was a good one: Australian oysters produce larger cultured pearls more quickly than Japanese oysters.

Cultured pearls are grown by opening the living oyster (in Australia, the silver-lip oyster, *Pinctada maxima*) and inserting a piece of mantle and an artificial "nucleus" into a cut made in the flesh of the oyster. The mantle is the lip of the oyster and it is this which produces the nacre, or pearl coating. The nucleus becomes the core of the cultured pearl. The right nucleus material is essential: the most commonly used being obtained from the shells of mussels occurring naturally in the Mississippi region of the United States.

A natural pearl is the result of the oyster dealing with an irritant, such as a grain of sand – or the nucleus. Although the oyster tries to eliminate the irritant, modern techniques ensure that over 80 per cent of the implants are successful and the nucleus stays in place. Failing to get rid of the irritant, the oyster uses the layer-building potential of the mantle to cover it. After six months, the oyster is taken out of the water and X-rayed to check that the nucleus has been retained.

A healthy Australian oyster will coat the nucleus in several layers of nacre each day, the pearl being ready about two years after implantation, when it is removed from the oyster and another nucleus inserted. Some pearl farm oysters may produce two good pearls in a lifetime. Only those that produce a good first pearl are implanted a second time and, rarely, some of these may go on to produce a third. After that, they're too old and the pearls too slow-growing so the final cycle is dedicated to producing half pearls. For this process several hemispherical nuclei are glued to the inside of the shell. At harvest time, the oyster must be killed because the half-pearls can only be removed by sawing them off the shell.

Kuri Bay, north of Derby, was named in honour of Tokuichi Kuribayashi who became the most influential person in the Japanese pearl industry following the death of Mr Mikimoto. The operation he established there is now part of Australia's Paspaley Group and is that company's largest farm in the region.

The first Kuri Bay pearls were produced in 1958 and in 1980 an 18 mm flawless, perfectly round pearl produced there was insured for $150,000. Pearls up to 20 mm are produced, but only very rarely.

■ The handful of superb pearls (below) is an example of the harvest for which Broome is famous. It takes almost two years for a cultured pearl to be ready for harvesting.

Another long-established Kimberley pearl farm is managed by Bruce and Alison Brown who took over the work of Bruce's father Dean, who with Bruce's brother Lyndon was a pioneer in cultured pearl farming in Australia. Their farm, at Cygnet Bay in King Sound, produced its first pearl in 1961. When Dean Brown died in 1980, his ashes were scattered on the headland overlooking the pearl leases he established.

Today, the greatest concentration of pearl farms is at King Sound, with six companies operating there. Paspaley Pearls with 4 of the 16 licences is the largest, followed by M. G. Kailis with three. Better management techniques mean that disease-induced mortality, like that which swept the industry in the mid-'80s, is no longer a problem. However, in the 2001-2002 season a parasite was discovered in some wild oysters and an emergency response plan was invoked to stop it spreading. Other recent problems for the Kimberley pearl industry included a drop in prices because of world oversupply and some cyclone damage to wild oyster stock.

Contrary to popular belief, the Broome pearl trade of the past had very little to do with pearls. A pearl was a very profitable bonus only for the lucky few. The real trade was in pearl shell, or mother-of-pearl (more commonly referred to by its initials, MOP). It was used mainly for buttons, cutlery handles and ornaments. In 1955, Australia was supplying 80 per cent of the world's requirements of MOP.

Commercial pearling commenced in Australia in the late 1860s at Shark Bay and Nickol Bay, WA. However by the 1890s, operations had shifted north and Broome was the centre of the Western Australian pearling industry. Most of the divers in those early days were Aboriginal. But they were soon joined by "Malays" – a term then used generically to describe anyone from Indonesia or Malaya – particularly after the Pearl Shell Fisheries Act of 1871 introduced some minimal safety standards to the industry. The new law prohibited the employment of women as divers: in those harsh times some had even been forced to dive in the final months of pregnancy.

These were the early days of "skindiving", when the divers regularly descended to depths of perhaps 18 m or more without breathing apparatus. Even when regulations absolutely limited skindiving to 13 m it was a rough trade and many divers didn't survive a season.

But technological progress produced a more insidious danger than sharks and overwork. Helmeted diving gear was introduced to the Kimberley between 1884 and 1887. It took some years before the cause of decompression sickness (which occurred all too regularly) was understood and "staged ascents" introduced to avoid nitrogen bubbling out of the body tissues after a diver surfaced. This is similar to the way bubbles form when the cap is removed from a bottle of fizzy soft drink. The syndrome is popularly known as "the bends" because it commonly occurs in joints like elbows and knees.

The industry was booming. Japanese divers had replaced Aboriginals and by 1903 Broome had a fleet of 300 pearling vessels, all taking shell from ever-greater depths. Between 1909 and 1917 Broome recorded 145 deaths from "diver's paralysis". Many other divers finished their days permanently crippled from the destructive effects of the nitrogen bubbles. Broome received its first (and the world's first) decompression chamber in 1913. The device is still on display in Bedford Park. By 1918 Broome divers were following Admiralty diving tables and the death rate had dropped dramatically.

Although pearl shell was the mainstay of the industry, a good quality pearl could make a pearler rich. The diver who found it also received a share of the profit. Such rewards were rare – only one oyster in thousands has a pearl and less than one per cent of those pearls are gem quality. Even so, some struck it rich.

The best natural pearl taken from the Kimberley oyster beds so far is the "Star of the West", a drop-shaped pearl about the size of a sparrow's egg. It was found in 1917 and was sold for £6000.

The "Southern Cross" is Australia's most famous pearl: it is a formation of nine pearls in the shape of a crucifix and it was found by a young boy cleaning shell near Broome in 1883. One of several stories about its origins tells how, when it was found, it was broken into three pieces and sold by the lugger skipper for £10. It was reassembled (with the addition of a ninth pearl to make the shape more balanced) and valued at £10,000 in 1924. It is now in the Vatican collection.

Plastic buttons came on the market after World War II and heralded the demise of the traditional mother-of-pearl button. By 1958, the MOP industry was in the doldrums. There had been ups and downs in the market before, but by 1960 Australian pearling was saved only by the advent of the cultured pearl industry.

Diving for oysters is still an integral part of the pearl industry. The oysters required for the pearl farms are collected from naturally occurring pearl beds by divers. Indeed, until 1974 most divers were still using the old-style diving suits with helmets. However, when it was established that a diver using lightweight hookah equipment could work more effectively, the Broome pearlers adopted the newer technology. Hookah resembles scuba gear except the diver doesn't wear tanks but relies on a hose link to tanks and a compressor on the vessel above. The luggers gave way to progress, too. Most pearling is now done from modern steel boats rather than the traditional wooden-hulled luggers.

Although more efficient, the steel ships, with their hookah divers, don't have the same mystique as an old lugger with helmeted divers.

Fortunately there are still a lot of copper helmets in shops, stores and museums around Broome and a few old pearling luggers to be seen. Although visitors can still buy pearl shell, the emphasis these days is on cultured pearls. In beautiful juxtaposition, Broome pearls are now found in settings alongside Argyle diamonds. Pearling techniques may have changed and Broome may no longer run on a schedule dictated by the movement of the pearling fleet, but the industry – worth around $200 million annually and by its very nature sustainable – remains very much a part of life in the Kimberley today.

■ The hemispheres on this pearl shell (above) are a sign that the oyster is nearing the end of its productive life. When a mollusc ages and its production of nacre slows, nuclei for inexpensive half-pearls are glued to the inside of the shell. When the nuclei are sufficiently coated, the oyster is killed and the half-pearls sawn off.

■ The traditional heavy diving helmet (opposite, top) was found in a Broome storeroom. Since Broome's last helmeted diver retired in 1975, helmets have become part of history. They were widely superseded by less clumsy hookah gear in the early 1970s.

■ Created by Spanish designer Carrera, the pearl pendant (opposite, below) set with gold and diamonds highlights the beauty of its precious components.

WILDLIFE AND PLANTS

There is no doubt that scenery, wildlife and Aboriginal culture are the Kimberley's main tourist attractions. It's impossible to travel through the region without being impressed by the distinctive plants and the variety of native animals one sees.

Most notable are the birds. In fact, dawn at the Marlgu Billabong (outside Wyndham) can be the most memorable experience of a trip to the north Kimberley. Here countless wildfowl are concentrated into quite a small area. Herons, black swans, pelicans, ibis, stilts, black-necked storks (jabirus), spoonbills, cranes and many varieties of ducks are just part of the passing parade. At this billabong, and at other waterholes, one may chance upon brolgas performing a mating dance that has much of the grace of a courtly quadrille.

There are some species of northern birds that impress by their sheer numbers. In the dry season, when burning off is common, every swirling column of smoke is full of black kites feeding on the insects borne aloft on the thermal currents. Flocks of budgerigars often sweep across the roads in the drier grasslands, then disappear in an iridescent green flash when their passage is interrupted by a car. Often trees appear to have erupted in dense clumps of large white blooms, which closer inspection reveals to be sulphur-crested cockatoos or corellas. (Black cockatoos are common, too, although not seen in such large flocks.) But the Kununurra sky darkened by an endless stream of magpie geese is the Kimberley's most imposing wildlife sight.

Rivers in the Kimberley are full of fish. Small black bream appear to be in every permanent waterhole in the north. The common insect-eating archer fish shoots water from its mouth with amazing accuracy to knock prey off overhanging branches.

The mammals and reptiles of the Kimberley are generally quite elusive, but wallaroos and several species of wallaby may be seen: trees near water can be festooned with flying-foxes during the day; snakes, frill-necked lizards, marsupial mice and bandicoots are present but shy. New species of reptiles are still being discovered in the Kimberley. On rare occasions, an emu or dingo may be seen.

Crocodiles
In May 1987, the Kimberley came under the world media spotlight when a visiting American model was taken by a crocodile near waterfalls on the Prince Regent River. This certainly highlighted the danger of approaching the Kimberley's most impressive inhabitant.

Filling the sky, a flock of hardhead ducks (opposite) flies from Marlgu Billabong. The hardhead flies faster than most ducks and can remain under water for periods of up to one minute. For many visitors to the Kimberley bird-watching, particularly around billabongs as the wet season ends, is a wonderfully rewarding experience.

"All crocs are territorial," Malcolm Douglas told me as we walked around his crocodile park in Broome. "But each has a distinct personality and some are more aggressive about it than others.

"Now Agro here won't take any encroachment lightly." Malcolm had a long wooden pole in his hand that he extended over the fence and across the placid waters of a pool. "Look what happens when I just touch the surface lightly." The pool instantly exploded in a thrashing frenzy, a seething mass of water and glistening ridges and teeth. It was my first real insight into what the final minutes of those who had gambled on swimming in crocodile-inhabited waters, and lost, must have been like.

There are two species of Australian crocodile: "salties" and "freshies". The freshwater crocodile (*Crocodylus johnstoni*) is almost universally regarded as harmless. It's certainly quite timid in the wild. Not so *Crocodylus porosus*, which grows much larger than the freshie and is quite ready to regard people as a meal. Some authorities encourage the use of the term "estuarine" rather than "saltwater" crocodile as this species can be found in fresh water 100 km or more inland. The two types are easily distinguished: a freshie has a much finer snout and, less obviously, a row of four large plates on the neck, immediately below the head.

Crocodiles are reptiles that have existed for some 200 million years, they are found throughout northern Australia, from Broome on the Kimberley coast to Rockhampton on the eastern coast of Queensland. During the late 1970s and early '80s there was heated debate about their numbers and whether we needed to be protected from them, or vice versa.

◼ Lashing the pool in a frenzy, a large saltwater crocodile (above) at Broome Crocodile Farm shows its displeasure when the keeper touches the water with a pole. Crocodiles are extremely territorial and any intrusion may be greeted by attack.

Holding one of his newborn charges (opposite top), adventurer and film-maker turned Kimberley crocodile farmer Malcolm Douglas shows how hatchlings are perfect crocodiles in miniature; every plate and feature is in perfect detail.

Holding one of his newborn charges (opposite top), adventurer and film-maker turned Kimberley crocodile farmer Malcolm Douglas shows how hatchlings are perfect crocodiles in miniature; every plate and feature is in perfect detail.

Clutching a flower between its teeth (left), a baby freshwater crocodile is surrounded by the pioneers of a new Australian industry: crocodile farming. Besides bringing commercial gains from both tourism and crocodile products, crocodile farming is adding considerably to our knowledge of this creature, whose ancestors survived for over 200 million years with little change.

Daunting in their saw-blade array, the teeth of this mature saltwater crocodile (below) are ideally suited to a diet mainly of mud crabs, turtles and, occasionally, birds and mammals.

Freshwater crocodiles have been protected in Western Australia since 1962 and salties since 1970 (in both cases Western Australia set the lead for other States) and the export of skins was prohibited by federal law in 1972. A rapid increase in tourism in the north and an increase in the number of saltwater crocodiles has increased the potential for tragedy. The best advice is: if a sign or a local resident says "don't swim", then don't. Nor should anyone consider stealing crocodile warning signs – doing so can be tantamount to manslaughter.

The growing number of crocodile farms in Western Australia, the Northern Territory and Queensland is a response to Australian saltwater crocodiles being transferred from Appendix 1 to Appendix 2 of the CITES agreement. CITES is the Convention on International Trade in Endangered Species of Wild Flora and Fauna. The more flexible Appendix 2 allows limited commercial use of wild stocks under close scrutiny. Besides providing handbags, shoes and steaks, the crocodile farms provide a useful base for scientific research and close, safe access to crocodiles for tourists.

Still, there is nothing like the thrill of seeing your first crocodile in the wild – from a safe vantage point. As a fisherman on the Wyndham wharf told me: "Everyone comes up here and they all want to see crocodiles. A few find out that the only thing worse than not seeing a croc while you're here is meeting one unexpectedly."

Barramundi

The opportunity to fish for barramundi is a lure for visitors to the Kimberley. It's high on the locals' list of sports, too. Barramundi is one of the world's great game and table fish, providing both a thrill in the catching and excellent eating. Like the estuarine crocodile, it

■ A solitary fisherman (above) tries for a catch at Ivanhoe Crossing, 8 km from Kununurra. A popular fishing spot, Ivanhoe Crossing is the first obstacle barramundi meet on their way up the Ord River; they must wait until enough water flows over the crossing to allow them to continue.

is found throughout northern Australia, from the Ashburton River in Western Australia to the Mary River in Queensland. Southern anglers must travel north to experience the excitement of catching "barra".

Tales of "barra" weighing in at up to 50 kg are legion, though a 1970s tagging survey in the Northern Territory found an average weight of 2.6 kg. Fishing expert Steve Starling says that amateurs should regard any barramundi over 8 kg as noteworthy and a catch over 20 kg as only an outside chance. The most popular fishing spots are along the Fitzroy River near Derby and the Ord River near Kununurra (especially at Ivanhoe Crossing). Remote, rarely fished areas may yield larger fish. However, the barramundi's unusual life cycle makes it highly vulnerable to overfishing.

The barramundi is highly adapted to the climate and seasons of tropical Australia. Between October and January barramundi make their way to the sea to spawn. The larvae develop into small fish in the salt water and then make their way up the river systems until the streams stop flowing. Obviously, high dam walls block this migratory path but, where

KUNUNURRA resident Bill Treasure (left) catches a barramundi below the dam gates of Lake Kununurra. Judged too small, it was released back into the river. Pelicans in the background, unhindered by bag limits, fished throughout the afternoon. Barramundi are particularly prone to overfishing. There are no female barramundi less than six years old so catching large fish takes a disproportionate percentage of females, reducing breeding potential.

A lone fan palm (above) is silhouetted against the red rocks of a gorge. The gorges of the Kimberley hold many surprises for first-time visitors. Deep, shaded clefts and cool waterholes encourage the growth of many palms, in stark contrast to the acacia woodland of the plains.

possible, the fish may proceed further upstream in the next Wet. At age three or four, they all mature as males and make their first return journey to the sea for the spawning season. Between the ages of six and eight some become female in a process called protandry. As all female barramundi are large, overfishing is a real threat.

The Fisheries Department of Western Australia, which has offices in Broome and Kununurra, is developing a plan to avoid this. A licence is not required for barramundi but there's a possession limit of five "barra" per person.

Plants of the Kimberley

It's probably true – visitors to the Kimberley have generally not been lured by the promise of vast and impressive displays of wildflowers. Yet the natural beauty of the Kimberley – one of the world's great wilderness areas – is partly the result of its own unusual flora. Home to a spectacular, abundant and diverse array of plants means that wherever you might be in the Kimberley you will be treated to magnificent colours and fragrances of a selection of seasonal wildflowers that, for much of the year, enhance the vast and rugged landscapes.

Roads that seem to stretch forever transport the traveller through extensive savannah grasslands. Dotted with the occasional abandoned vehicle that gives every appearance of having been there almost as long as the arid deserts themselves, the spinifex-and-scrub landscape takes on the peculiar guise of a strange primitive cemetery as the masses of termite mounds come into sight. Boabs – nature's own caricature – create yet another unique Kimberley image.

Look beyond the big picture, however, and the world of Kimberley flora presents itself. Vast open plains lead to hidden valleys where *Livistona* and *Pandanus* palms make you believe you're in tropical paradise; bougainvillea and frangipani colour the streets of many of the towns; the Australia-wide genus *Grevillea* is found here in diverse forms; and the brilliant yellow of the wattle and kapok trees against clear, deep blue skies and red-dirt roads make both a striking image and a lasting memory.

The wattle is one of the country's most distinctive trees – a symbol of Australia. Species of *Acacia* are distributed throughout tropical and warm temperate areas, so it comes as little surprise to find them throughout the Kimberley. Acacia, as well as eucalypts, dominate the Kimberley flora. Acacia shrublands on sandy soils occur in abundance in parts of the region's south-west. *Acacia tumida*, or pindan wattle, is a particularly attractive feature of the Kimberley. During the dry season, when the deep blue skies light up the landscape and the roads are a rusty red that is every bit as intense as the sky, the tiny soft yellow blooms combine in clusters on the wattles to create a picture of primary beauty.

The north Kimberley, dominated by savannah woodland, is home to many species of *Eucalyptus*. The stark white gums are particularly striking when seen against dramatic backdrops of rugged ranges and cloudless blue skies. In complete contrast, the woollybutt, *Eucalyptus miniata*, could be described as almost dainty. With its deep orange pompom-like

flowers, golden-tipped, the woollybutt is a plant of delicate beauty, although it does not possess a fragrance of equal beauty and it is sticky to the touch.

Another of Australia's favourites, *Banksia*, can be found throughout Western Australia, with many species thriving in the Kimberley. Easily recognised by its cylindrical flower spikes, it is the Banksia's colour and leaf formation that varies from one species to another. *Banksia dentata* is one species that flourishes in the Kimberley, growing either as a shrub or a small tree.

The growth of lush palms in a region of the country that also contains some of its most arid desert areas strikes many visitors as extraordinary. The *Livistona* and *Pandanus* palms are two such plants – typical flora of the Kimberley's gorges and valleys.

The fan palm, *Livistona eastonii*, is common in the Mitchell Plateau, but venture off the roads and into any of the spectacular gorges with their plunging waterfalls and secluded waterholes and you're likely to discover palm-fringed creeks and groves, creating a shady oasis in an otherwise hot and dry environment.

Like the palms, cycads at first sight might seem a surprising feature in the Kimberley, yet certain species, such as *Cycas basaltica*, are widespread in the northern Kimberley region. Extremely hardy plants, the cycad family possesses a palmlike beauty, with the plants'

A wonderful blaze of colour (above) on otherwise arid ground is one of the rewards of travel in the Kimberley. The parakeelya, a succulent annual plant, copes well with the harsh conditions and blooms readily. Its fleshy leaves hold moisture that has been known to help livestock survive cross-country travel.

■ The woollybutt, *Eucalyptus miniata* (above), and the caustic bush (above right) are two of the commonly occurring plants of the Kimberley. Perfectly adapted to the long dry season they bring colour to the landscape and provide welcome shelter from the sun for birds and small animals.

fronds promising shade nearby. The imposing *Cycas armstrongii* is a remnant of the flora that covered Gondwana, the southern supercontinent, in the age of dinosaurs.

Several of the 40 or more species of *Calandrinia* that are native to Australia are found in the Kimberley. These succulent, ephemeral plants show considerable diversity in arid and semi-arid regions. The fleshy leaves offer life-supporting moisture, known to provide sustenance to Aboriginal people (who know the plant as parakeelya) and to keep livestock going through cross-country travel when no free water is to be found. *Calandrinia* species display brilliant and dramatic splashes of colour in arid areas, with softer and less conspicuous colours in the wetter regions.

Boabs

Boabs are your constant companions in the Kimberley: silvery giants with huge trunks and stubby branches growing in a cluster from the top. Their expressive postures make it hard not to humanise boab trees – particularly when there are a couple of bulky parent trees surrounded by a brood of skinny offspring.

In Australia the boab is found only in the Kimberley and a neighbouring area of the Northern Territory. It is the sole representative here of the genus *Adansonia*. There are nine species in the genus, seven of which are found only on the island of Madagascar, off the east coast of Africa. The baobab or monkey-bread tree (*Adansonia digitata*) is widespread in tropical Africa. Boabs and baobabs were probably neighbours when the continents were joined together as Pangaea. However, another theory suggests that both species came from Madagascar around 190 million years ago, after nuts were swept across the ocean and deposited on these distant shores.

Boab is a truncation of the African "baobab", the spelling preferred by the *Macquarie Dictionary*, but in the Kimberley the Australian variant is universally used. The botanical name of the boab is *Adansonia gregorii*, named after the noted explorer Augustus Gregory. The tree was first described in 1857 from specimens obtained by the botanist Ferdinand von Mueller on the Augustus Gregory expedition of 1855.

Today the photographers who bewail the difficulty of finding a roadside boab that has not been defaced by graffiti carved into the bark may not realise this is the continuation of a long standing tradition. The first European to describe the tree was Phillip Parker King, who referred to "the gouty habit of the stem". His crew carved "H.M.C. Mermaid 1820" on a boab near the mouth of the Prince Regent River. Thirty-five years later, Augustus Gregory carved a message for following members of his party into a boab on the banks of the Victoria River.

The boab flower is creamy white and about 10 cm long. The large fruit (up to 25 cm long and 15 cm in diameter) is initially green and hairy but becomes brown and furry. Inside, dozens of black seeds are packed into the pulp. The boab is deciduous, losing its leaves in the dry season to retain moisture stored in the soft, spongy wood.

The map below shows the natural distribution of boabs in the Kimberley. This distinctive form of a familiar sight is hard to miss in this region, so characteristic of the Kimberley landscape.

Boabs grow quickly and may live for more than 1000 years – one in Africa is estimated to be 5000 years old! These enormous trees can have a circumference greater than their height. Local history says that particularly large boabs near Wyndham and Derby were used as overnight cells by police officers transporting prisoners. However, prisoners were probably chained to, not put inside, the trees.

Kimberley Aboriginals used the boab as an all-purpose provider. The pith of the seed is edible (with high protein and vitamin C content) and was sometimes crushed to a powder and made into a bread. Moisture can be extracted from the wood or roots, the gum makes a convenient glue and the bark can be used as twine.

These days, boab nuts serve mainly as artists' canvases sold as souvenirs, especially around Wyndham, where every store seems to carry them. The smooth, brown fur of the nuts is carved, with varying degrees of skill, by Kimberley artists.

Probably one of the best places to see a large collection of boab trees of all shapes and sizes is at Derby airport. With their grotesque limbs and distended trunks silhouetted against the setting sun, they remind one of Ernestine Hill's description of the boab in *The Great Australian Loneliness*: "A Caliban of a tree, a grizzled, distorted old goblin – a friendly ogre of the great North-west."

Strange bulbous forms are characteristic of the boab (opposite), so it's not surprising it came to be known as the "bottle tree." The bottle tree of Queensland is no relation. Boabs don't grow as tall as African baobabs but can reach a larger circumference up to 16 m.

Etched into the brown, velvet-textured surface of boab nuts (below), scenes of outback life take on an extra dimension. As it matures, the boab fruit changes from green and hairy to a brown, woody shell that becomes the artist's canvas. Inside are scores of hard, black seeds in a firm, pithy matrix.

TRAVELLING THE ALL-WEATHER ROAD

The 1034 km journey from Broome to Wyndham along the Great Northern Highway – or the black-top as it is popularly known – is a trip to remember. The route passes through not only the main towns of the Kimberley but also through the many different landforms that so strongly characterise the Kimberley region.

Broome

Walking the bustling streets of Broome or standing at a bar listening to tales of tourist development and soaring housing prices, it's hard to imagine that the town was long held to have no potential at all. Indeed, after Broome was gazetted on 27 November 1883, the man after whom it was named, the Governor of Western Australia, Sir Frederick Napier Broome, wrote to the Colonial Secretary to complain: "I believe the town named after me ... is likely to remain a mere 'dummy' townsite inhabited by the tenants of three graves ... My present idea is to have the name cancelled." He didn't get his way and, in an ironic twist of fate, few have any idea after whom the famous town was named.

For much of Broome's existence, the town has been known as "the Port of Pearls". When plastic buttons largely replaced pearl shell after World War II and the pearling industry went into decline, so too did Broome. Even so, in 1954 Broome (with a population then of about 1100) was still being described as a "rip-roaring shanty town". Today Broome's resident population is around 13,000 and the town has not lost all of its rowdiness – although now the crowds around town are more likely to be tourists than pearl divers.

Broome has one important feature that is lacking in all other Kimberley towns: it possesses sandy beaches. Cable Beach and the other strips of pristine sand stretching north towards Beagle Bay may be the basis of Broome's future growth. The development in the 1980s of the luxury Cable Beach Club and Roebuck Bay Hotel marked a significant turning point for what was once a shanty town. Today visitors have many places to choose from when they stay in Broome including self-contained apartments, hotels, bed-and-breakfasts, caravan parks and backpackers' hostels. For those who have travelled overland from the east, some time spent having a beach holiday at Broome is wonderfully refreshing.

One of the many attractions of the beach here is the "Stairway to the Moon", a phenomenon that can be seen under clear skies at full moon. As the tide recedes hundreds of metres, exposing rippled sand

A camel ride along Cable Beach (opposite) remains an enduring memory for many visitors long after their holiday in the Kimberley is over. The beach, stretching for 22 km, adds its special character to the feeling of vast, open spaces so typical of the Kimberley. Magnificent sunsets light the sky here, contrasting with dramatic storm clouds as the Wet approaches.

flats, the reflection of the moon on the ridged surface creates a fanciful stairway effect. Many visitors time their trip to coincide with this memorable sight.

Cable Beach takes its name from the international telegraph cable that came ashore here from Java which, in turn, was linked to London. In 1889 the new line supplemented the original London–Australia link through Palmerston (now Darwin). A transmitting station, complete with tennis court and a separate billiards room, was built in Broome; it is now the town's courthouse. With its large verandas and sloping roof, the building remains a superb example of northern Australian architecture. It is also a buzzing centre of activity on Saturday mornings with the courthouse markets now famous throughout Australia.

Broome's cosmopolitan past is evident in the revitalised Chinatown, with its footpath cafes and pearl showrooms and in the historic cemetery where the gravestones bear witness to the diverse origins of the town's early residents. The Aboriginal, Indonesian, Filipino, Malay, Japanese and Chinese workers in the pearling industry have certainly left a rich, cosmopolitan legacy for the town.

After Broome was bombed in World War II, there was strong local anti-Japanese feeling but in 1952 the Australian Government authorised a specific exemption to the "White Australia Policy" so that Japanese divers could return to Broome to revive the pearling industry. Balancing the memory of those who died in the air-raids, Broome's Japanese cemetery is a poignant reminder of the Japanese contribution to Broome and pearling. The Shinju Matsuri (Festival of the Pearl) in Broome is an annual acknowledgement of the bond between Broome and the pearlers of Japan.

Broome today is a most unusual country town. There are very few small towns in Australia (or anywhere else, for that matter) that have several shops stocking jewellery among which are single pieces worth tens (even hundreds) of thousands of dollars. In Broome it seems that every second shop sells pearls. The casually dressed holiday-makers must have more money than their shorts and T-shirts suggest: the exquisite Broome pearls on display sell well despite the price tags.

There is a cultural richness to Broome that appeals to every visitor. New colonial-style buildings and the sleepy Chinatown, the rambling Streeters & Male store from Broome's first days, Sun Pictures (a commercially operating open-air picture theatre dating back to 1916) and pearling luggers tied up at the old jetty, all contribute to the feeling. The attractions of the town and its surrounding areas are many. In the sandstone at the water's edge at Gantheaume Point, and revealed at low spring tides, are the petrified footprints of a carnivorous dinosaur that lived 130 million years ago. Less extreme tides reveal the corroding hulks of flying boats sunk in the air-raid of 1942. There's even the faint promise of hidden treasure: an extremely unlikely legend has it that William Dampier buried a sea chest here when careening his vessel and there is the more tangible mystery of the "Flight of Diamonds". The latter concerns an aircraft that came near Beagle Bay on an evacuation flight from Java during World War II. A box of diamonds that had been

The street is crowded as patrons leave Sun Pictures (top), Broome's open-air cinema, after the Saturday night show. Sun Pictures first opened in 1916 and has operated continually ever since, changing little over the years. Chinatown (above) is always a drawcard for visitors with its lively cafes and the numerous shops offering an amazing selection of pearls. Broome's cosmopolitan style is closely linked to the development of the pearling industry here.

on board was discovered later by a beachcomber who is reputed to have distributed many of the precious stones to friends and supporters.

Broome is the Kimberley's southern gateway and the region's seaside resort. Huge sums are being spent developing tourism. About 200,000 travellers arrive each year and not all of them leave. Throughout its history many casual visitors to Broome have decided to stay. As a result, this town continues to grow faster than anywhere else in the Kimberley.

The shoreline at Roebuck Bay, Broome (below), offers stretches of sandy beach and dunes against a backdrop of the ever-present red rocks. The chance to enjoy some time at a beach entices many visitors to the town.

Distances can be daunting in the Kimberley. The road sign (above) shows how much country lies ahead for those setting off on a cross-Kimberley drive. Fuel, water, tools and spare parts are a vital part of any trip.

Myall's Bore near Derby flows into a stock trough (right) which, at 120 m, is long enough, it's been said, to slake the thirst of 1000 head of cattle at the one time. Keeping cattle in good condition before shipping to market can be difficult in the Kimberley climate.

Broome to the Derby turn-off

Much of the drive from Broome to the junction with the Derby Highway – a distance of some 178 km – passes through rolling plains of classic savannah country. Later, thick acacia scrub in turn gives way to majestic boab trees and thousands of termite mounds, before the landscape changes again and the numerous creeks and rivers that form part of the vast Fitzroy River floodplain begin to dominate the scene.

There is a turn-off to Langey Crossing and Telegraph Pool some 145 km east of Broome and both of these locations offer some of the best barramundi fishing in the Kimberley. Not surprisingly, however, these locations are also home to some of the Kimberley's largest saltwater crocodiles, so swimming is not recommended. Dogs have been taken by crocodiles in the area on numerous occasions.

At the Willare Bridge Roadhouse, which is about 166 km east of Broome, the Great Northern Highway crosses the Fitzroy River and travellers can stop here to enjoy a bite to eat and take the opportunity to refuel. The road junction offering the route either to Derby or to Fitzroy Crossing is some 12 km east of Willare. Derby is a further 42 km away along the Derby Highway.

As you near Derby, Myall's Bore, which feeds into what is believed to be the longest stock trough (120 m) in the southern hemisphere, is just off the highway on the right. Nearby is

A huge and ancient boab tree, popularly referred to as the prison boab tree, which has a girth of 14.7 m. It is an Aboriginal site of some significance and you are asked not to approach it too closely. Visitors can, however, visit the Spirit of the Wandjina Art Studio at the Mowanjum Aboriginal Community, just a short side trip along the Gibb River Road after turning off the Derby Highway.

Derby

The relaxed lifestyle generally found in the Kimberley is a tonic to city dwellers and it is a particularly appealing feature of Derby – the town that extended credit to the first pastoralists. Derby (pronounced "Durby" not "Darby" as in England) has long been regarded as the market town for the west Kimberley. Broome (gazetted on the same day, 27 November 1883) may have had the flash pearlers but Derby was the port of the west Kimberley and the service town for the pastoral and grazing industries. It was named after Lord Derby who, like the Earl of Kimberley, was a Secretary of State for the Colonies.

Unfortunately, Derby's port on King Sound has always proved difficult for shipping. There are savage tidal rips at the entrance and both the channel and wharfside are virtually dry at the lowest extreme of the enormous tidal range – the greatest range anywhere in Australia. On King Tide day in May, the difference between high and low tides is a staggering 11 m. Unlike early vessels, modern ships are not designed to sit on their keels and that, combined with silting problems in the Derby channel, has caused port use to decline markedly since the early 1980s.

The first Derby jetty was opened in 1885, two years after the woolclip from Yeeda station was washed away by the tsunami (giant wave) caused by the eruption of Krakatau. In 1902, the horse-drawn tramway was extended 4 km across a causeway to the jetty, a great advantage in moving cargo. That original jetty stood for 79 years before finally being replaced in 1964. The "new" wharf seemed fated to become just an historic landmark and fishing platform but it is now being used to load ore into barges for transport to the bulk carriers that moor in deeper water offshore.

Derby developed quickly at the time of the Halls Creek gold rush but it soon had to compete with the new port of Wyndham that opened up closer to the goldfields in 1886. The town has always been a communications centre: the first airmail service in Australia was between Geraldton and Derby in 1921, largely overcoming the communication difficulties created by the inaccessibility of this northern region.

An important institution in Derby today is the hospital, which was once the largest in the Kimberley and has become integrated with the operations of the Derby base of the Royal Flying Doctor Service. Near Yeeda station, 40 km to the south and the first enduring grazing property to be established in the west Kimberley, is the $64 million Curtin RAAF Base which for a time doubled as a commercial airport and has potential as an international passenger airport.

Reflections in a shop window (below) mirror the wharf end of the Derby township. When this photograph was taken the house across the road, built in the traditional style of northern Australia, was being renovated. Like many buildings in Derby, it has a boab tree as a neighbour. The four-wheel-drive vehicle out the front is representative of many such vehicles that form a large proportion of Kimberley traffic.

Wet-season rains frequently cause a sudden, dramatic increase in the flow of Kimberley rivers. Rivers that have been reduced to nothing more than a chain of pools during the dry season flow strongly again, pushing debris ahead of the surging water. The swollen Fitzroy River (below) experiences flooding during most wet seasons, joining with the nearby Brooking Channel to create a sea of water.

Under threatening skies a road train (opposite top) hurtles along the "black top", as the Great Northern Highway is known, near Fitzroy Crossing. Road trains are an invaluable means of transporting stock but, with as many as three trailers, they are large vehicles and motorists need to take care when overtaking. Sealed roads are rare in the Kimberley. A graded gravel road (opposite below) is more usual, but these roads can become severely corrugated at times.

Derby's population of around 5000 is an open-hearted community living in an open-plan town of wide, boab-shaded streets. For travellers it's the stepping off point for the Gibb River Road and the many natural features along the way, including Tunnel Creek and Windjana Gorge. The majestic coastline of the Buccaneer Archipelago, a short plane flight to the north, reveals the tidal phenomenon of the Horizontal Waterfalls. Scenic cruises in this area are becoming increasingly popular out of Derby. Locals continue to see Derby as the long-standing administrative and service centre for the west Kimberley with a solid future in tourism.

Derby to Fitzroy Crossing

Travelling east on the Great Northern Highway the road from Willare to Fitzroy Crossing passes through open plains country before eventually giving way to acacia scrub and bauhinia woodland closer to Fitzroy Crossing. Extreme caution should be exercised on this road, particularly when driving at night and facing the lights of oncoming traffic. Each year unfenced stock cause accidents, some fatal, on Kimberley roads. Investment in a good set of spotlights is highly recommended before driving in the Kimberley.

Approximately 78 km along the Great Northern Highway from the junction with the Derby Highway the road crosses the Erskine Range, which marks the beginning of "Bunuba" country, centre of one of the main Aboriginal language groups in the Fitzroy Valley area. The climate in this region can have quite an impact on travel. During the dry season the route

is frequently marked by bushfires and during the wet season one must exercise care at all floodways and creek crossings.

Fitzroy Crossing provides an opportunity for travellers to again refuel and rest before the 293 km stretch to Halls Creek. The historic "Crossing Inn" on the old township site remains a popular tourist attraction. In 1997 it celebrated its centenary as the oldest Kimberley hotel on its original site.

In the middle of the dry season, the 1500 people who live in Fitzroy Crossing township must sometimes feel besieged by tourists. More than 50,000 people travel through the town each year and 30,000 of them turn off the highway to visit Geikie Gorge, 17 km to the north. Since the "new" bridge opened in 1974, the centre of Fitzroy Crossing, one of the Kimberley's fastest-growing communities, has shifted from the original townsite towards the highway. The community's main centre lies at the foot of the central Kimberley hills. To the west, the Fitzroy floodplain spreads towards the mouth of the river where it runs into the vastness of King Sound.

Turning onto the Geikie Gorge road reveals the predominantly Aboriginal community of Fitzroy Crossing spreading over several kilometres along the banks of the Fitzroy River. The river continues to dictate life here. Named after Robert Fitz-Roy, the captain of the *Beagle* when it carried Charles Darwin before its voyages along the Kimberley coast, the river's catchment area is 45,300 sq. km (compared to the Ord's 46,200 sq. km). When the river is in flood, more than 98 million cu. m of water may flow past Fitzroy Crossing each hour (enough to fill Sydney Harbour in about five hours) and the Crossing Inn, situated right on its banks, is regularly inundated somewhat restricting its operations. For most of the other half of the year the river is merely a series of waterholes. In this fluvial "feast-or-famine" environment, water for the town is supplied from a bore.

Fitzroy Crossing took a decade to come into being as the great Australian triumvirate: a police station, telegraph office and pub. The latter has been in existence, in one form or another, since the 1890s and like all country pubs is often the hub of local activities. A stroll through the local Pioneer Cemetery on Stuthorp Road gives today's visitor a fascinating glimpse into the long history of this remote place. The whole settlement remains vital today. The Sunday "session" at the Crossing Inn is legendary throughout the region – the open-air dance floor is packed with a cheerful crowd from the town and surrounding stations. Minus the rock music it could be the Kimberley any time in the past hundred years.

Fitzroy Crossing to Halls Creek

There are no roadhouses or stores between Fitzroy Crossing and Halls Creek so it's essential to make sure you have everything you need before setting out. This stretch of road is one of the most rewarding of those on the Great Northern and, for the more adventurous, offers stunning gorges and caves to the highway's north and scenic desert country and escarpments to its south. Ninety kilometres to the east of Fitzroy Crossing, in the Lawford

Shafts of sunlight (above) deep in the gorges and tunnels of Mimbi Caves contrast with the deeper, shadowy caverns also found here. Situated in the Devonian limestone that makes up the Lawford Range the caves are attracting attention for their interest to scientists as well as tourists. Taking advantage of occasional sunlight a hardy plant (right) has become established deep within a narrow gorge.

Range, the Mimbi Caves and Galeru Gorge are spectacular sites to visit. The Lawford Range, like the Napier and Oscar ranges further west, forms the remains of what was once a massive undersea reef system. As sea-levels receded the reef was uplifted and it is now regarded as a marine fossil site of international significance. The cave system still remains largely uncharted and is one of the largest in Western Australia. The local Aboriginal people conduct small-scale tours here; bookings can be made only through the Fitzroy Crossing Tourist Bureau.

Halls Creek offers a totally different feel to that offered by Fitzroy Crossing and it too has some remarkable local attractions. The ranges to the town's east contain some stunning gorges and a short, 45 km drive along the Duncan Road will take travellers past China Wall and the popular waterholes of Caroline's Pool, Palm Springs and Sawtooth Gorge. Palm Springs is a permanent waterhole and offers a cool respite from the intensity of a harsh tropical sun. Further east lies some of Australia's best cattle country; to the south lies the spinifex and termite mounds of the Tanami Desert. The Bungle Bungle Range is 162 km by road to the town's north-east and Wolfe Creek Crater is 100 km to its south. A scenic flight over both of these dramatic parts of the landscape is a memorable experience.

One shouldn't expect modern Halls Creek to show any signs of the boom town that did so much to establish the Kimberley. The township moved from the site of original settlement to its present position in the early 1950s to allow for further expansion, to take advantage of a more reliable water supply and to give the town room for an airstrip. Although the town had a population of 2000 or more at the time of the gold rush, Old Halls Creek's had only 300 residents by the time it was moved to its present site – laid out as a string of shops along the highway and a grid of streets to the south. An interesting story of life in gold rush days is told in the statue of a local character known as "Russian Jack" that stands in the main street. There is still the feel, here, of an outback town on the edge of the ever-present desert. Many of the local people still speak their own Aboriginal languages and are happy to share their stories and their knowledge of plants and animals with courteous travellers.

Apart from the old Post Office building, the wooden beams and mud brick walls of the original goldmining town have crumbled away, but the new Halls Creek is an increasingly popular tourist destination helped by the energy and drive of the Shire and residents who live there. Several secluded swimming and picnic spots are within an easy hour's drive of the town and fossicking for gold along the creek beds is another drawcard. Besides the old goldrush town and nearby Wolfe Creek Meteorite Crater Reserve, Halls Creek is a gateway to the Bungle Bungle Range at Purnululu National Park. Economically, there's potential for new mining development including rare earths and platinum-group elements. There is a goldmine at Lamboo station and a new nickel mine at Fletchers Creek. Halls Creek Shire's many indigenous artists, some of whom are nationally recognised, contribute to the works on view at the art centres at Balgo, Warmun and on the main street of town.

In several ways, Halls Creek is unusual. It is the only Kimberley town on a road junction and it is the largest one to be located far from the coast (Kununurra is close to the mouth of the Ord River). This town, with a population of 1600, most being Aboriginal, marks the point where Highway One is joined by Duncan Road and, just west of town, by the Tanami Track coming from Alice Springs past Wolfe Creek Meteorite Crater. Its location and altitude (400 m above sea-level) give Halls Creek a more pleasant climate than that experienced by other towns in the Kimberely. It has less rain in the wet season and experiences generally cooler nights throughout the year.

Viewed from the air, Halls Creek (below), which is the Kimberley's most inland town, is displayed in its setting of flat terrain. In 1948 the townspeople voted to move from the original makeshift town to the current site, which has the advantages of a good water supply, room for expansion and is close to the airstrip and highway.

■ The statue and plaque (above), which are displayed in the main street of Halls Creek, recall the story of a local character, generally known as "Russian Jack" who, during the days of the gold rush displayed true Aussie mateship. Using a wheelbarrow to carry his injured friend he walked more than 300 km to seek medical help.

Halls Creek to Kununurra

The drive north from Halls Creek passes through what must be some of Australia's most spectacular roadside scenery. Here the Great Northern Highway leaves the plains that stretch to the east of Halls Creek and turns north and north-east, passing through primarily range country for the majority of the 359 km drive to Kununurra. Each year during the Wet, this stretch of road is closed for periods when floodwaters make passage unsafe: in fact, numerous vehicles are lost each year when travellers misjudge the depth and/or rate of flow at creeks and floodways. A number of floodways have been replaced by two-lane bridges, but some potentially hazardous crossings remain. It is strongly recommended that, if there is any uncertainty, travellers first walk a crossing. A good rule of thumb is that drivers should not attempt to drive a river crossing if the water depth is above their thighs or if the rate of flow prevents a safe walk across. Even after the Wet, travellers should exercise caution at creeks and floodways as remnant wet-season debris such as tree branches can cause considerable damage if hit at speed.

The Aboriginal community of Warmun, approximately 166 kilometres north of Halls Creek, is the home of nearly 1000 people, mainly Aboriginals. Refreshments and fuel are available here at the Turkey Creek Roadhouse – a good opportunity to take a break.

Heading north from Turkey Creek, the scenery becomes more spectacular with every kilometre. Range country gives way to granite country, characterised by thousands of large granite boulders, some larger than a two-storey house. The recently established Doon Doon Roadhouse, about 120 km south of Wyndham, is a new opportunity to buy fuel or refreshments. From here the landscape is punctuated by many escarpments. To the east lies Lake Argyle, formed when the Ord River was dammed, and one of the most spectacular natural sites in the Kimberley – the Ragged Range. Concealed by the Blatchford Escarpment the Ragged Range is an assortment of tall red pillars of conglomerate sandstone where ancient livistona palms can be found growing in seemingly impossible places. The range's dramatic landforms and the stunning colours to be seen here at sunset can only be viewed from a concealed lookout that lies a couple of kilometres in off the Great Northern Highway some 110 km to the south of Wyndham.

North of the Ragged Range the country changes again. To the east lie the plains of the Dunham Valley and then the unbroken wall of the Carr Boyd Ranges. A drive along this stretch of the Great Northern Highway in February when water is plentiful reveals a stunning variety of unnamed cascading waterfalls, which become permanent pools in the Dry, and, in the distance, a white sandy beach that seems to point to the existence of an inland sea rather than the black soil plains and range country between which it is situated. Some 55 km from Wyndham, the Great Northern and Victoria highways meet: to the north-west lies Wyndham and to the north-east Kununurra.

Extreme care is necessary when driving at night here because much of the 45 km drive from the turn-off is unfenced. Some 15 km from Kununurra the more intrepid can choose

■ Black Rock Falls (above), while only a seasonal waterfall, is spectacular, the water tumbling more than 50 m into a plunge pool below. The falls are a memorable sight after heavy rain and can be seen from up to 20 km away in nearby Kununurra when in full flow.

to follow a gravel road to the popular local spots of Black Rock Falls and Middle Springs. While waterfalls themselves are only seasonal, permanent pools provide a welcome respite from the heat that pushes well into the 30s, even in the Dry. The road into Kununurra crosses the diversion dam bridge (the wall below Lake Kununurra) which itself acts as a popular fishing spot for local barramundi anglers. As with all prime barramundi locations close to the saltwater, the area below the diversion dam is frequented by some of the Kimberley's largest saltwater crocodiles.

Like Canberra many decades earlier, Kununurra was designed and built to a plan. It was created in the early 1960s to service the Ord River Irrigation Area but it has since developed as a regional centre in its own right, replacing Wyndham as the centre for the east Kimberley.

Travellers get quite a surprise coming into Kununurra from the Victoria Highway, particularly if they have driven up from Halls Creek. The town of just over 5000 people is well-planned and neat. Other Kimberley towns just grew over the years and their town plans are largely the result of historical accident. However, Kununurra existed on a drawing board long before the first house or road was built. While new development has seen the township spill across to the south of the Victoria Highway, the town is still largely centred around a central horseshoe-shaped road – Coolibah Drive. The ends of the horseshoe join the Ivanhoe Road, which goes out to the farms of the Ord River Irrigation Area. Most of the shops and offices are within a block of the southern side of Coolibah Drive and radial roads lead off to the residential streets.

Inevitably, Kununurra is modern. In fact the sight of so many new buildings and numerous conventional suburban houses seems quite incongruous in the Kimberley. The town's central position in Kimberley affairs makes it an ideal base for exploring the region and several hotels, motels and caravan parks have arisen to service that need. From here it's possible to take a conventional plane, float plane, helicopter or 4WD trip down to the Bungle Bungle Range, visit Lake Argyle, the irrigation area near Wyndham, or head down the Gibb River Road. Kununurra also has the regional headquarters of the Department of Conservation and Land Management (CALM), which administers all the national parks of the Kimberley.

The top of Kelly's Knob, north of the built-up area, provides an excellent view of the township and the patchwork fields of the irrigation scheme, particularly at sunset. Throughout the hot days of the tourist season, black kites can be seen soaring along the ridge top within metres of the lookout.

Many visitors find Kununurra a surprise in the Kimberley landscape. There is no feel of a frontier town here, of a place that grew up on adversity and became strong through self-reliance. Rather, it feels very much like the rest of Australia, just like any other country town. But that is also Kununurra's main attraction. It is a place in which to shop and rest and it provides a touchstone of normalcy that makes visitors realise how special the Kimberley is and how unique its other towns really are.

Kununurra to Wyndham

The drive from the Kununurra turn-off to Wyndham along the Great Northern Highway is truly stunning. Huge boab trees and, during the wet season, 3 m high spear grass, stud a landscape dominated by the towering red and orange fortress of the Cockburn Escarpment. In the late afternoon during the Wet, bolts of lightning can often be seen striking nearby hills. During the Dry, the smoke from bushfires and the ever-present dust reduce visibility markedly. Some 20 or more kilometres along the way, the seasonal Grotto Falls are worth stopping for. After the passage of a monsoonal deluge during the Wet, the falls thunder 30 or so metres into a permanent pool below. Nearby, the soothing bubbles of the aptly named but seasonal Soda Creek offer a more relaxing alternative for the less adventurous.

Standing on Five Rivers Lookout on the summit of the Bastion Range, about 300 m above Cambridge Gulf, allows a magnificent view of Wyndham's port. From that point you can trace the course of the Ord, King, Pentecost, Forrest and Durack rivers as they flow into the gulf. It is a beautiful view and puts the town of Wyndham in perspective: a small town clinging to the strip of land between the hills and the edge of Cambridge Gulf. The serene and picturesque setting belies the town's economic ups and downs.

Hit badly by the closure of the meatworks in 1985, Wyndham, as the northernmost town in Western Australia, now profits as the port for the burgeoning live-cattle trade to Asia and

■ A keen angler (left below) pursues the goal of many such enthusiasts in the Kimberley – a barramundi on the line. The spillway at the Kununurra diversion dam offers good fishing but can be treacherous. Fishing is generally only allowed further downstream.

■ Ragged Range (opposite) has the potential to become one of the Kimberley's most recognisable natural features. Located to the north of the Bungle Bungle Range it offers a spectacular mix of escarpment country, tall palms and conglomerate domes.

Encircled by two linked sandstone plateaus, the Cockburn Range towers more than 600 m above the surrounding plains and is one of the Kimberley's most imposing sights. Scree slopes at the base of the escarpment contain many examples of "ripple rock" suggesting that the area was once in a tidal zone.

the Middle East and exports from the increasingly productive Ord River Irrigation Area nearby. The Asian economic downturn of the late 1990s had potentially serious outcomes for the port but the wharf is still viable and busy with the export of live cattle and sugar and the import of nitrate. Still the main port for the east Kimberley region it retains much of the atmosphere of an old Kimberley town. Boabs line the main street and most of the action centres around the pub. The old courthouse in the port area is now the town's museum. A number of developments currently in the planning stage should help stimulate what is a wonderful part of the Kimberley.

Wyndham is really two towns about 5 km apart and linked by a sealed road that skirts the edge of the Cambridge Gulf mudflats. Most of the 800 people who live here have houses at what is still almost universally referred to by locals as the "Three Mile", while the main points of interest for tourists are clustered around the port. The reason for the two towns is topographical: as the population grew there was no room to accommodate the newcomers at the port, which is squeezed between the water's edge and a steep sandstone ridge. To solve the problem, settlement was established at a point on the track about three miles (5 km) inland from the port. In 1968 the Three Mile Settlement officially became part of Wyndham.

The gold rush at Halls Creek provided the impetus for the establishment of Wyndham. It was declared a townsite on 2 September 1886 and named Wyndham by John Forrest (later Lord) after the son of Lady Barker, wife of Sir Frederick Napier Broome, Governor of Western Australia. A shortage of fresh water at the port saw settlements and camps spring up at the 20-mile post and at three-mile intervals between the 12-mile post and the port. The route was used regularly as miners came for supplies and, later, pastoralists brought cattle down for shipment to Fremantle or South-east Asia. Apart from the "Three Mile", these communities no longer exist. After the gold rush the town languished until 1919 when the meatworks opened. Until its closure in November 1985 the works provided one of Australia's most unusual and grisly tourist attractions: large saltwater crocodiles waiting at the outflow of the abattoir's blood drain. Today most croc-spotting is done at the crocodile farm, fittingly located on the site of the old meatworks. Still, Wyndham's limited appeal as a bathing spot is not enhanced by the baleful stare of a big "salty" occasionally sunbathing below the wharf. A huge crocodile statue, over 4 m high and 20 m long, stands at the entrance to the town.

Wyndham is surrounded by rivers and water and is unique in being the only town in the Kimberley not supplied from a bore. It relies on Moochalabra Dam for its water. The water is pumped about 20 km over the tidal flats to storage tanks near town. Another waterhole fulfils a more picturesque function: Marlgu Billabong, a bird sanctuary 15 km from the "Three Mile", is home to pelicans, brolgas, black-necked storks (jabirus), cranes, herons and innumerable magpie geese. At dawn, the enthusiastic birdwatcher can come close to many species that are only seen from afar elsewhere in the north. Not far from the billabong Parry's Creek Farm provides cabins and camping facilities.

Viewed from the air the town of Wyndham [left] seems to be restricted by its location between Cambridge Gulf and the Bastion Range. A separate section of the town, 5 km from the port, is now the main residential area. Visitors arriving in town are greeted by an enormous statue (below) of a saltwater crocodile. Real "salties" can be viewed at a nearby crocodile farm.

TRAVELLING THE GIBB RIVER ROAD

From the comfort of Australia's large cities and the well-developed areas of the east coast the whole of the remote, empty Kimberley seems like a wilderness. However, the truth is that some of the Kimberley is generally as readily accessible as anywhere else in Australia. The towns of Broome, Derby, Fitzroy Crossing, Halls Creek, Wyndham and Kununurra are linked by the Great Northern Highway, an all-weather road, and one can generally travel right across the Kimberley without difficulty. Wet season rains can, however, cut parts of the Great Northern for many weeks at a time, although some major bridgeworks by the Department of Main Roads over the last few years have done much to reduce delays. There are some areas of the Kimberley, however, that are seen only by the most intrepid traveller. The adventure involved in reaching these places can be just as important as the destinations.

The "alternative route" across the Kimberley is the 700 km long Gibb River Road that runs from Derby to Wyndham. After the first 65 km of sealed road from Derby the road is unsealed (but well-formed enough for road trains) right through until it rejoins the Great Northern Highway 48 km out of Wyndham. Between November and April intending travellers should check with the police at either end before setting out, as rain can swell the creeks and make the road impassable during the wet summer months. And, as with any form of travel off the highway in the Kimberley, motorists should ensure they have fuel, spare tyres and parts, as well as food and water enough to last through any emergency. Fuel requirement calculations should take into account the likelihood of some rough, slow going.

Along the route from Derby to Wyndham fuel is available at Imintji (220 km) and Mount Barnett Roadhouse (300 km). There are camping facilities at Windjana, Bell and Manning gorges and accommodation and camping facilities at Mount Elizabeth, Ellenbrae, Home Valley and El Questro. Accommodation (but not camping) is offered at Imintji, Emma Gorge and at Mount Hart by prior arrangement.

Some of the mystique of the Gibb River Road has disappeared in recently as more and more people now travel the road. Accordingly, although traffic drops dramatically after September, those travelling during the peak months from May to August should not expect a wilderness experience. In fact, the pressure of increased numbers of visitor is becoming cause for concern and many station owners are moving to ban roadside camping to provide for better control and management of what is a very fragile environment.

■ Motorists on the Gibb River Road pass through a gap in the Napier Range (opposite). Long stretches of open country along this road are relieved by some imposing rocky escarpments and rugged ranges. The trip from Broome to Kununurra is more than 1000 km; along the way there is plenty of opportunity to explore the heart of the Kimberley.

The rocky outcrop on Napier Downs station known as Queen Victoria's Head (below) is a familiar landmark for those who know the Gibb River Road well. Seen at sunset the rock face glows with the warm colours so characteristic of the Kimberley landscape.

Derby to Lennard Gorge

After leaving Derby and turning off onto the Gibb River Road, the road continues across the coastal plains before gradually climbing onto the uplands of the central Kimberley. Gradually the open plains recede and the way is flanked by vegetation, which includes many impressive boabs. The surrounding country is also dotted with the thousands of termite mounds that are characteristic of Kimberley scenery. Visitors seeing this landscape for the first time marvel at the memorable scenes created by the combination of boabs and termite mounds.

The turn-off to Windjana Gorge and Tunnel Creek is 119 km from Derby and that road, if followed beyond Tunnel Creek, eventually brings you back onto the Great Northern Highway 42 km west of Fitzroy Crossing. But from Derby the country remains fairly flat as the Gibb River Road passes through the stations of Napier Downs, Kimberley Downs and Meda – home to some of the best cattle country in the Kimberley.

Mount Hart station (above), about 200 km north-east of Derby, began as a pastoral lease in 1914 and operated as a cattle station until 1987. It is now Mount Hart Wilderness Lodge, open through the dry season. It's accessible from the Gibb River Road on a picturesque 50 km drive through the King Leopold Range. The homestead is typically Kimberley and is in the middle of expansive lawns and a cool garden.

■ Seemingly unending, savannah woodland stretches across a vast area of Beverley Springs station north of the Gibb River Road on the eastern side of the King Leopold Ranges. A flight over this country reinforces its enormous size and the isolation of many homesteads.

Some 130 km from Derby, the road passes through a gap in the Napier Range that is known affectionately as Queen Victoria's Head, due to the apparent "likeness" of a rock formation near the road. The Napier Range is part of a Devonian Reef system that was created some 350 million years ago and which extends for a distance of some 350 km from Napier Downs Station. The range runs to the south-east, eventually petering out about 100 km to the east of Fitzroy Crossing.

The dramatic red granite structure of Mount Amy is clearly visible five or so kilometres to the west as the road begins to enter the foothills of the King Leopold Ranges. Some 7 km beyond the turn-off to Mount Hart a track off to the right leads travellers to within a kilometre or so of the top of Lennard Gorge. While the track was passable right through to the top of the gorge until fairly recently, severe erosion has now made the last kilometre or so impassable. The walk, however, is well worth the effort. At the top of the gorge, the Lennard River drops over a 20 m waterfall into a beautiful deep pool that is home to two Mertens water monitors. Further downstream the river cuts through a narrow chasm, only a few metres wide. Care should be taken at the top of the falls; a dry grey lichen can act as a treacherous slippery surface for the unwary.

Imintji and the gorge country

A little more than 20 km north along the Gibb River Road from the Lennard Gorge turn-off, another side trip tempts those who have a love of nature and a little time to spare. The seasonal track into Bell Gorge goes off to the left and runs for some 30 km. This track is generally only accessible during the dry season; the Western Australian Department of Conservation and Land Management closes it off until after the Wet as soon as the first rains make passage along the track impossible. At the 20 km mark Silent Grove, the primary campground used here, is an attractive place to stop. Bell Creek campground is 10 km further on but sites there are limited in number and intending campers must book well ahead to avoid disappointment.

Like all the gorges and waterfalls along the Gibb River Road, Bell Gorge has its special qualities. A one-kilometre walk from the car park brings visitors to the top of a waterfall and, by crossing over Bell Creek at the top of the waterfall, it is possible to climb around and down to the base of the falls and enjoy a swim in a large pool at the bottom. During the Dry, however, travellers should not expect to have the falls to themselves.

After this side trip, the roadhouse at the Aboriginal community of Imintji, set against the backdrop of the King Leopold Ranges, offers the first chance to refuel and to buy basic food items since leaving Derby.

North of Imintji the road passes through the one-million-acre (4000 sq. km) cattle property of Mount House, and the turn-offs to Beverley Springs station (45 km to the west) and Old Mornington Camp (100 km to the east). Both properties, while offering only marginal cattle country, are sites of some of the most spectacular Kimberley scenery.

Bell Creek Gorge (left and above) is one of the most spectacular gorges in the west Kimberley. The creek tumbles through a series of cascades and pools as it falls some 100 m through a cleft in the King Leopold Ranges. Walkers are rewarded with some beautiful glimpses into verdant gorges lit by a golden glow from the sandstone walls.

Accommodation is available at both stations. West of Beverley Springs lie the spectacular gorges of the Charnley and Isdell rivers while Old Mornington, which was recently acquired by the Australian Wildlife Conservancy, is home to the beauty of the Diamond Gorge, where there is great barramundi fishing, and Sir John Gorge.

Approximately 65 km beyond Imintji lies Galvans Gorge. From the car park a short walk of about one kilometre brings visitors to a set of falls which, towards the end of the Dry, slow to a trickle. There is a popular swimming hole here overlooked by a boab tree at the top. Some Aboriginal art from the Wandjina period can be seen in an overhang to the right of the waterhole as one looks towards the falls. It is not difficult to pass a couple of hours at this beautiful spot. Overhanging ferns and vegetation provide welcome shade from the hot Kimberley sun and you can relax in the cool waters below the falls.

Mount Barnett Station to Gibb River Station

A short drive of about 14 km beyond Galvans Gorge brings you to Mount Barnett station and the cooling waters of Manning Gorge. Mount Barnett station is an Aboriginal owned working cattle property and fuel, basic food items and souvenirs are available from the roadhouse. There is a campground close to the waters of Lower Manning Gorge, although a permit is required before proceeding to the camping ground. If you plan to arrive after the roadhouse has closed, you should ring the roadhouse beforehand as a barrier gate will otherwise make access impossible. A further 2 km upriver from the camping ground, visitors can enjoy the beauty and tranquillity of Manning Gorge Falls. The walk is well worth the effort and gives an insight into the beauty of the country further west.

A little more than 30 kilometres after leaving Mount Barnett a left hand track, itself some 30 kilometres long, leads to the Mount Elizabeth Station homestead. This station, established by Frank Lacey, is run by his son Peter and Peter's wife Pat. To the west of here lies some of the most dramatic scenery in the entire Kimberley and, depending upon the time of year, scenic flights are available for those wishing to get a view of this spectacular and inaccessible wilderness area.

Much of Mount Elizabeth station, like most of the country along the Gibb River Road – especially that to the west – is dominated by brutal and inaccessible sandstone country that is punctuated by deep gorges and ravines and escarpment country. Only the most experienced and fit bushwalkers dare tackle this area, which must surely rate amongst the most rugged country anywhere in the world. Frank Hann, during his epic trek of 1898, noted that "only a man greedy for trouble would want rougher country to travel over". At any time of year walking in this country is difficult, although during the build-up and in the wet season, when the heat is most intense, the country becomes like a furnace. The intense heat of the sun is made even greater as it is radiated by the sandstone. In this landscape there is no escaping the heat.

Travelling north from the Mount Elizabeth turn-off the road comes to the Hann River crossing. The Hann is a major river and the road here is impassable during the Wet. In recent years the Hann has been the starting point for white-water rafting expeditions down the Hann and Fitzroy rivers to Fitzroy Crossing.

This stretch of road passes through eucalypt-dominated woodland. Thirty kilometres after the Mount Elizabeth turn-off, a track to the left leads to the homestead of Gibb River station, which was established by the pioneering Russ family. But for long stretches the road passes through untouched, uninhabited country.

The speed at which one can travel along the northern part of the Gibb from Mount Barnett to its junction with the Great Northern Highway is largely a function of traffic volume and the time that has elapsed since the last cut of the Main Roads graders. If the graders have passed through recently it is not uncommon for travellers to move along at the speed limit or thereabouts. If graders haven't been seen for some time, and traffic has been

■ Sister Scholastica (above), seen here riding past the chapel on the mission's motor-tricycle, is a regular sight around the Kalumburu commuity, the northernmost settlement in Western Australia. With Kalumburu's large vegetable garden and extensive community the trike is invaluable as an all-purpose, lightweight vehicle. The first Catholic mission in the area was established in 1908. It shifted to Kalumburu in the 1930s.

■ Galvans Gorge (opposite top) is only 600 m from a car park a short distance off the Gibb River Road but it feels much more isolated. The beauty of the surroundings, the refreshing swimming hole and the lush vegetation make this an ideal place to take a break.

■ Opportunities to use a phone (opposite) are infrequent for those travelling in remote areas of the Kimberley. Some homesteads have these facilities for visitors, as well as camping and, sometimes, the opportunity to buy fuel.

■ Seen from the air the Mitchell Falls (above) make a dramatic sight as they tumble off the plateau. The river itself was named after Sir James Mitchell, Premier of Western Australia. The falls and plateau were named much later, taking their names from the river.

heavy, road corrugations can slow travel down to no more than 20 or 30 km/h an hour and sometimes cause considerable damage to vehicles. Broken springs and axles on this stretch of road are not uncommon when the road is in this state, although some find this hard to comprehend when they have passed through immediately after the Main Roads graders.

Mitchell Plateau Road

For those who want to experience the even more remote parts of the Kimberley, deviations from the Gibb River Road will be enticing. About 411 km from Derby the turn-off onto the Kalumburu-Mitchell Plateau Road leads to a real outback experience. Permission must be obtained from the community at Kalumburu before going there and accommodation must be arranged in advance through the monastery. Permission is not automatically granted but, if it is, the effort is well worthwhile. The old mission buildings, with the well-kept orchards and gardens behind, are beautiful and there is a lot of good fishing in the area. Father Ansar also runs tours of a museum that has been established in Kalumburu and these, for most, are a highlight of any visit to this remote community. On the far side of the unpaved airstrip the wrecks of some aircraft destroyed in Japanese air-raids during World War II are still to be seen. Kalumburu is 267 km from the Gibb River Road. It usually takes several weeks after the end of the Wet before the road is graded and reopened. After some particularly severe wet seasons access has been delayed until June. The last 40 or so kilometres before Kalumburu can be quite rough as the road, punctuated by sheets of rock, passes through rugged sandstone country.

To the east of the Kalumburu Road lies the spectacular and inaccessible Drysdale River National Park and the towering feature of the Carson Escarpment. The escarpment is one of the most impressive sights in the entire Kimberley and dominates the skyline for 200 km running in a predominantly northerly direction before coming to an end near Cape Londonderry on the north Kimberley coast. The Drysdale River National Park can only be reached by helicopter or on foot meaning that only the most experienced and fit bush-walkers should plan to visit the area.

About 172 km along the Kalumburu Road the turn-off to the Mitchell Plateau, a region of great significance to the indigenous people, branches off to the left. William Easton, who led a government expedition across the plateau in 1921, named the river after Sir James Mitchell, a Premier of Western Australia. When extensive bauxite deposits were discovered there in 1965 by a mineral company's exploration team, expedition leader Ken Malcolm named the plateau after the adjoining river.

The track onto the Mitchell Plateau is definitely for four-wheel-drive vehicles only. There is a good riverside campsite, which is very popular and can be crowded but it does have permanent fresh water, about 2 km on the right after you cross the King Edward River. A short distance after crossing the river – prior to the turn-off to the campgrounds – a bush-track leading off to the left leads to a spectacular rock-art gallery. About 500 m past the mining camp, 57 km along the track, there is a turn-off to the left that leads to Camp Creek, which is 8 km ahead in an open valley. This is a popular camping base for exploring the other features of the plateau. Four and a half kilometres north of the mining camp is the turn-off to Mitchell Falls – you can drive to Mertens Creek, 12 km from the turn-off and there is a 45-minute walk to the falls. It's recommended that you allow all day for the trip to the falls because the return walk can take from four to six hours. Although there is camping here, sites are limited. Camp Creek is a better option.

The last major side trip on the way to Walsh Point and the termination of the road at the edge of Port Warrender is the Surveyors Pool, which is surrounded by impressive white cliffs of King Leopold sandstone. If you are thinking of camping here, bear in mind that no water is available on the walk in, although water-bottles can be filled at the pool and

■ Tracks on the Mitchell Plateau, shown on the map below, allow exploration of remote parts of the Kimberley. All of these roads are likely to be impassable during the wet season.

carried out. The turn-off to the Surveyors Pool is 24 km after the mining camp – you can drive 6 km but must walk the last 4 km.

Jack's Waterhole to Wyndham

Jacks Waterhole was closed to the public following the wet-season floods of 2002, although there are plans to reopen the area as soon as facilities and access can be re-established. Previously, the waterhole was a beautiful area in which an array of birdlife provided a stunning opening to the cool clear mornings of the dry season.

Located on Dawn Creek, Ellenbrac station, with its two beautiful billabongs, offers pleasant canoeing and camping. The station was one of a number that have been recently acquired by private sector interests associated with the Kimberley Foundation: an organisation dedicated to both the preservation and study of rock art throughout the region and the area's pristine wilderness.

Many of the best sights in the Kimberley can be seen only from the air. A special highlight of the Kimberley is the line of Elgee Cliffs along the western bank of the Chamberlain River. Although these run parallel with the Great Northern Highway for about 125 km (the road is at least 50 km to the east), they are hidden by intervening ranges and can be seen and fully appreciated only from the air. Imagine a very straight river stretching to the horizon with a high steep bank rising along its length to the sharply defined angle of the crest. That's the view of Elgee Cliffs from an aircraft flying at about 5000 feet. Even among the considerable scenic grandeur of the rest of the Kimberley, these cliffs stand out. El Questro Wilderness Park, nestled in the valley, looks very much like paradise – it certainly has a very dramatic backdrop.

The road reaches the top of the Pentecost Range about 90 km beyond Ellenbrae and 2 km further along there are spectacular views of the flat mesas of the Cockburn Range and down into Cambridge Gulf to the north. If it's possible to plan your timing, the approach to the Cockburn Range is best taken in the evening, around sunset. Travellers are greeted with what can be a spectacular light show as the escarpment - dramatic sandstone cliffs at the southern end of the range - changes colour in a crescendo to brilliant, fiery red. Home Valley station, one kilometre down a fork to the left, charges an admission fee that gives access to station-style accommodation, camping and basic amenities. Fuel is unavailable but there are telephone facilities and some good fishing. Nine kilometres from Home Valley the road comes to the Pentecost River.

During the Wet, the Pentecost River Crossing typically acts as a natural barrier to traffic along the Gibb. It marks the end of the tidal confluence from the salt waters of nearby Cambridge Gulf. During the Dry, but depending upon the severity of the immediately preceding Wet, the crossing dries to a depth of half a metre or so making crossing generally uneventful: although, it is not uncommon for the more ambitious two-wheel-drive adventurers to find themselves in difficulty if care is not taken. There is bush camping near the

■ Evening at the homestead at El Questro Wilderness Park (above) is a time to sit around the campfire and listen to some story-telling.

■ The Pentecost River crossing (opposite left) is quite manageable in the dry season but hazardous in the Wet. The crossing marks the highest point of the tidal reach; salt water from Cambridge Gulf flows back to here.

crossing but the river is tidal here and is home to saltwater crocodiles so, despite its tempting coolness, the water is not for swimming and care should be exercised with any ints. Eighteen kilometres further north along the Gibb a turn off to the right takes you to El Questro Wilderness Park where there is camping and drinking water.

El Questro Wilderness Park is a testament to the vision and energy of its creators, Will and Celia Burrell. Established in its current form in 1991, the park offers an incredible diversity of attractions which can easily occupy a week or more of visitors' time. The park is characterised by hot thermal springs, deep gorges and droplet waterfalls and a wealth of rock-art from the Wandjina period. For those wishing to get an aerial perspective of what is also a million-acre (4000 sq. km) cattle property, the presence of a helicopter stationed at the park for scenic flights offers travellers additional opportunities to appreciate the grandeur of the Cockburns and the stunning beauty of the nearby Chamberlain, Pentecost, Durack and Salmond rivers (many of which flow through untouched sandstone gorges of their own). Not far south of El Questro limited station-style camping and bed and breakfast accommodation is available at the Indigenous Corporation-owned Home Valley station.

Back on the Gibb it is only a 34 km drive to the junction with the Great Northern Highway and then little more than the same distance on to the end of the route at Wyndham.

■ In the remote south-eastern part of El Questro Wilderness Park the beautiful Miri Miri Falls (above) are a hidden treasure. A helicopter ride is the easiest way to visit the falls but an alternative, an all-day cross-country walk, has its own rewards.

THE KIMBERLEY COAST

"When Australian Geographic put Susan and myself on the Kimberley coast in 1986 it really was the middle of nowhere," Michael Cusack recalls. "Today there are aircraft overhead, vessels passing by and oyster floats in just about every lovely bay. It may no longer be the longest undefiled coastline on earth but William Dampier would still recognise it.

"I still get the same feeling when I go there. There's a remarkable sense of place. Of course the site near Kunmunya Mission where we lived for a year means most to us. I first returned more than 10 years after our year in the wilderness and Susan returned in 2000. In the 2003 dry season we visited with our children."

The Kimberley coast may appear timeless but it is far from static. The huge tides that create two-way cascades and giant gales provide a daily pulse and the flow of seasons establish an annual rhythm. On a millennial scale, the place where Australia's first settlers stepped ashore during the last Ice Age now lies hundreds of kilometres offshore.

One feature that hasn't changed since I first visited the Kimberley 20 years ago is the lack of access to the coast by land. There are just three towns on the Kimberley coast: Broome, Derby and Wyndham. Elsewhere only four other tracks give vehicular access to the coast: the road to Kalumburu (from which an offshoot leads to the coast at Mitchell Falls), a track to Oobagooma north of Derby and the road from Broome to Cape Leveque.

Fortunately, it is becoming increasingly easier to explore the coast by boat. Tourist interest in the Kimberley has grown steadily in the past decade and that is particularly true of the coast. So the islands and bays that were once the domain of local fishermen and adventurous yachties can be visited on the scheduled voyages of several larger vessels. As landings and tours have been refined in response to visitors' interests, some coastal sites have become "must sees". All along this coast there is stunning scenery and many opportunities to explore ashore to see superb examples of Aboriginal rock art.

Travelling north

Broome is the southernmost port of the Kimberley and a natural departure point for travel along the Kimberley coast. For travel in the other direction the northern departure point is either Wyndham or across the border at Darwin. Most voyages from Broome turn right out of Roebuck Bay to head north along the shore of the vast peninsula known as

■ Though Broome's most notable feature is Cable Beach the region's best beach, some of the waterfront near town on Roebuck Bay (opposite), is more typical of the Kimberley coast. Here is that wonderful juxtaposition of red cliffs and blue sea that characterise the colours of this coast so well. Few roads lead to this coast so the best way to explore it is still by boat.

■ Changes in ship-building techniques have had a very direct effect on Kimberley shipping. A deep-hulled vessel (above) is left high and dry by the great Kimberley tidal range. Most modern vessels are not designed with enough strength to rest on their keels so they avoid this coast. Some multi-hulled passenger vessels, however, are an integral part of coastal tourist trade.

■ Protruding above a mass of greenery on the red soil at the northern tip of Dampier Land, Cape Leveque lighthouse (opposite) marks the western entrance to King Sound. Accessible by road, sea or air, it's about 16 km from both Lombardina Mission to the south and the pearl farm at One Arm Point. The 195 km drive from Broome to Cape Leveque is over rough, unformed sandy roads that soon become impassable in wet weather.

Dampier Land. But some sail due west for Rowley Shoals. These excellent examples of atolls rise some 500 m from the Australian continental shelf. There are three atolls: Imperieuse Reef, slightly the largest at 18 km by 10 km; Clerke Reef in the middle; and Mermaid Reef, the northernmost. The reefs are coral wonderlands with large fish and 200 species of coral. Most of the area falls within the Rowley Shoals Marine Park that attracts divers seeking a range of excellent dives. However, it is not without its challenges. The considerable tidal range exposes the coral walls at low tide and covers all but the sandy islets of Imperieuse and Clerke reefs at high tide.

If one sails north from Broome towards Cape Leveque, there are some other interesting islands much closer to the coast than Rowley Shoals. These are the four sandy islands on a limestone and coral base that make up the Lacepede Islands Nature Reserve. The group was named by Baudin, on his voyage of exploration in 1801, after Count Lacepede, a French politician and naturalist whose son was a member of Baudin's expedition. Decades later, between 1876 and 1879, there was a guano mining industry here that employed 150 people. In a strange historical footnote this industry was the subject of a diplomatic dispute between the

United States of America and Britain after the islands were claimed under the Guano Island Act of US Congress. Today the islands are most notable for the turtles and seabirds that nest here. It is the main Kimberley nesting site of green turtles, which come ashore each night from October to March. The islands have the largest colonies of brown boobies in the world and the largest colonies in the Indian Ocean of the lesser frigatebird.

Cape Leveque marks the beginning of the western entrance to King Sound. Above a sandy beach stands a headland of dramatically red rocks that glow in the late afternoon light. The cape is capped by a lighthouse and was named after the hydrographer of the *Geographe* that visited here in 1803. On the northern side of King Sound the Buccaneer Archipelago, a maze of almost 1000 islands, is a rewarding area to explore. It has been economically rewarding too: iron ore has been mined here, on both Koolan and Cockatoo islands, since 1951. Yampi Sound lies between the islands and the mainland. The red islands with white sandy beaches are spectacular enough but the huge 12 m tides create another feature known locally as the "Horizontal Waterfall" of Talbot Bay. This phenomenon occurs because a quartzite escarpment on the sea floor has been breached and the soft siltstone behind it has been eroded. As the tidal flow passes through the breach the escarpment becomes a dam wall over which water cascades, first one way then the other, on each turning tide.

At one of the many other deep indentations along the coast, the tidal show is more conventional but no less spectacular. Secure Bay, a quite large tidal body of water, is linked to Collier Bay and the open sea through a narrow gap that is aptly named The Funnel. Water cascades through here as the tide ebbs and flows. Nearby Walcott Inlet has been proposed as a national park, to be linked with King Leopold Ranges Conservation Park. Raft Point, to the north, would also fall within the proposed park. Visitors to this part of the coast come ashore at a beach below two high bluffs – distinctive landforms that can be seen

■ The two freshwater outlets into Secure Bay (above) are King Creek and Humbert Creek. They enter a pristine waterway that seems to well deserve its name as coastal vegetation flows down to tidal flats and tranquil waters. However, from the sea the mouth of the bay appears impenetrable as the whole bay must drain and fill through the narrow mouth aptly named The Funnel. For the mariner the nearby Buccaneer Archipelago (right) is not much less hazardous as its islands, headlands and peninsulas resemble a maze, even from the air.

from afar. At the top of the saddle between the bluffs is a rock gallery of Wandjina figures, perhaps the most unearthly of all Aboriginal art.

Bays, reefs and reserves

Doubtful Bay, a little further north, was the site of an optimistic venture by 19th century settlers that, in retrospect, was doomed to failure. Like Camden Harbour and Cape Villaret to the north this was the site of a failed sheep farm in one of the first of several endeavours by Europeans to settle the Kimberley in the 1860s. All fell victim to the extreme climate, isolation and Aboriginal resistance.

Montgomery Reef, some 15 km offshore from Doubtful Bay, was named by Phillip Parker King after Andrew Montgomery, the surgeon on the *Bathurst*. The reef extends over an area of 400 sq. km and in some places sandy islands have become established and even support mangroves. The mere description of the reef's tidal changes should serve as a warning to mariners. At high tide the large internal lagoon disappears while at low tide the reef stands as much as 4 m above sea level.

St George Basin, which has also been proposed as a marine park, is clearly distinguished by the two flat-topped mountains at the northern end that King, exploring in 1820, patriotically named Mt Trafalgar and Mt Waterloo. On the south-eastern side of the Basin is one of the most distinctive features in the Kimberley. Prince Regent River, which runs

Sheep Island (left), a lonely islet near the early settlement of Camden Harbour, served as the community's graveyard. Its beautiful setting and isolation remain unchanged.

The Horizontal Waterfall (below) is one of the most remarkable features in a region littered with oddities. Geology and tide combine here to create a dramatic cascade at sea.

The 50 m high waterfall, King Cascade (above), plunging past quite dense vegetation into the Prince Regent River is a favourite spot for visitors though tides present a challenge. It is also a place touched by tragedy as it was here that American model Ginger Meadows was taken by a crocodile in 1987 as the rock ledge on which she was standing was inundated by the rising tide.

dead straight for about 100 km between high cliffs created by block-jointing of King Leopold Sandstone, flows into the sea here. The river is navigable for more than 30 km and numerous tributaries run into the river at almost precise 90 degree angles. About 40 km along the river, King Cascade, which still appears exactly as King sketched it in 1820, is a favourite destination for visitors to the coast. The relatively untouched nature of this area helped it gain the status of a UNESCO World Biosphere Reserve, to maintain the flora and fauna of the region. Public access is restricted to the 630,000 ha Prince Regent Nature Reserve. A further disincentive to exploration is that this is the site of the most recent fatal crocodile attack in Western Australia, which took place in 1987.

The path of early mariners

Careening Bay provides a chance to come into direct contact with King's Kimberley coast exploration. The bay takes its name from King's need to repair the 84-ton *Mermaid* in September 1820. He wrote: "The leaky state of the vessel had been gradually increasing; leading me to fear that the injury received at Port Bowen had been much more serious than we had contemplated ... We were fortunately upon a part of the coast where the tides had a sufficient rise and fall to enable us to lay her on shore without difficulty." The crew put up a copper plaque during the 16 days they were here. It had disappeared when King returned the following year in the *Bathurst,* but the ship's name carved into the trunk of a boab is still visible today. It simply reads "H.M.C. *Mermaid* 1820". Allan Cunningham, the naturalist with the expedition, had time to do extensive collecting here and the species he found included the frill-necked lizard, which he named *Chlamydosaurus kingii* after King.

Many people consider Prince Frederick Harbour, the next deep harbour to the north, to be the most scenic part of the Kimberley coast. Green vegetation and towering red cliffs up to 200 m high mark the entrance to the Hunter River where King found fresh water and decided that it was "a discovery so valuable, that the river was thought worthy of a name and it was called after my companion Mr Hunter". That was James Hunter, the surgeon on the *Mermaid*. The tributary on the northern side of the river is Porosus Creek, named for the saltwater crocodile, *Crocodylus porosus*. Mt Anderson at the top of the creek is 480 m high and has massive terraces dropping down to the sea. Ships may use this harbour as the departure point for helicopter flights across to Mitchell Falls some 50 km away.

The most notable island in the Bonaparte Archipelago is Bigge Island. Legal history students will be familiar with the name: King named it in 1820 after "John Thomas Bigge, Esq., His Majesty's late Commissioner of Inquiry into the state of the Colony of New South Wales". It's a rugged island made up largely of barren quartzite and is populated by rock wallabies. The greatest attraction for most visitors to Bigge Island is the chance to see the amazing Aboriginal rock art here. The images depicted include scenes that reflect early European visits, such as sailing ships and figures smoking pipes. The Wunambal people who created this art have also painted Wandjina figures, distinctive for their huge haloed heads. These figures represent Kaiara spirits, which are believed to control the weather and even generate cyclones.

The next cape to the north is Cape Voltaire, named by Daudin in 1802 after the French philosopher and man of letters. Nearby Krait Bay is a link to one of the memorable moments of World War II. It was surveyed by the tiny Australian vessel the *Krait* as a depot for raids on Japanese bases in Asia and some old fuel drums are still to be seen there. The *Krait* sought safe mooring here after its renowned raid on Japanese-occupied Singapore.

At the head of Admiralty Gulf is Port Warrender, which was King's last port of call. While he was here, King found that rats had made substantial inroads into both his water and food supplies, so he decided it was time to set sail for Timor.

Rounding the north coast

Some of the names at the most northern edge of the Kimberley coast have a direct relationship with Arctic exploration. Parry Harbour, for example, contains both Fury Rock and Hecla Island. William Parry took the remarkably strong vessels *Hecla* and *Fury* on two unsuccessful attempts, between 1821 and 1824, to find the long-sought North-West Passage from the North Atlantic to the Pacific Ocean north of Canada. Modern mariners may be excused for thinking there was another rationale behind the naming of Fury Rock: a sailing guide to the area notes that the rock is awash at high water. Troughton Island to the north of Cape Bougainville has been used as a facility for the offshore oil rigs further to the north.

Perhaps Phillip Parker King was considering an application to the treasury for future expeditions when he named Vansittart Bay after an earlier Chancellor of the Exchequer. He gave Jar Island on the western side of the bay its name because he found shards of pottery there. They had probably been left after visits by Macassan sailors who came here seeking beche-de-mer long before Europeans came ashore. Other legacies of these early visitors are rock hearths from their cooking fires and even tamarind trees that are not native to the Kimberley. Above the beach at the northern end of the island is some rock art in the form of those strange, elongated representations known as Kimberley Dynamic or, formerly, Bradshaw figures, as well as some hand stencils.

On the eastern side of the Vansittart Bay visitors can walk over a sand-dune to see the wreckage of an aircraft that crashed on 28 February 1942, during World War II. The six crew members were all rescued a few days later. A little further to the north-east is the northernmost point of the Kimberley coast, the low rocky headland of Cape Londonderry at 13°44'S. It's not a place to sail close to for a better look: there are reefs extending seawards from the point for several kilometres. The cape was named after Robert Stewart Londonderry (1769–1822), the 2nd Marquess of Londonderry.

King George Falls are a spectacular sight, dropping over perpendicular sandstone cliffs more than 100 m high. They lie about 12 km up King George River and may stop flowing towards the end of the dry season. The bay at the mouth of the river is variously known as

One rarely comes face to face with history but at the "Mermaid" tree on the Kimberley coast one encounters a fundamental moment in the history of northern Australia. The letters "H.M.C. Mermaid 1820" that are carved on the boab tree some 200 m along the tidal creek that flows into the bay were carved during a 16-day sojourn here on that first survey of the Kimberley coast. The *Mermaid* was purchased for the expedition by Governor Lachlan Macquarie. The solid teak vessel was built in Calcutta and was 84 tons, 56 feet long and had a 9 foot draft

King George Falls (right) are the impressive conclusion to the navigable reach of the King George River. The river is navigable for 6 nautical miles upstream and for much of this voyage the river runs between high sandstone cliffs. At the end, the river in full spate can be seen plunging over the 100 m cliffs from the later stage of the wet season into the early stage of the dry season, around early May, although the flow may have ceased completely towards the end of the dry season. There are rock pools at the top of the falls that can be reached by a walking trail.

The enduring memory of a voyage along the Kimberley coast is of sandy beaches that may be bordered by cliffs preventing access to the interior, such as at this site in the Bonaparte Archipelago (opposite top). These beaches change dramatically in size and shape with the ebb and flow of the tide.

The Berkley River (opposite below) cuts deeply into the escarpment as it flows to the Kimberley coast. The river, which has its source in the Drysdale River National Park, enters the sea near Cape St Lambert.

King George Bay or Koolama Bay. The *Koolama* was a ship of 4000 tonnes owned by the Western Australian Government that was bombed off Cape Rulhieres on 20 February 1942. The ship sent an SOS to Kalumburu and Aboriginal guides took most of the people from the ship to safety on an overland journey of more than 100 km. The skeleton crew who stayed with the ship sailed the vessel to Wyndham but it was sunk near the wharf during a subsequent air-raid. The wreck is still visible at very low tides.

This is an area for transportation traumas. Just to the south-east is Seaplane Bay where German aviators Hans Betram and Adolph Klausmann were forced to land in 1932. They were eventually rescued by a local Aboriginal, but they had waited 38 days before being found.

The last spectacular river gorge on the Kimberley coast is the mouth of the Berkeley River, which spills into the sea just south of Cape St Lambert. As one heads east towards the Northern Territory border from here the landforms are flatter and less dramatic. The mariner must now make a choice – whether to continue to the north-east across the Joseph Bonaparte Gulf to the bright lights of Darwin, or to turn south into Cambridge Gulf and travel down to Wyndham.

NATIONAL PARKS

The Kimberley is an area of scenic splendour that is uniquely Australian. Here boabs and eucalypts, spinifex-littered buttes and mangrove-lined tidal inlets combine into one fascinating whole. However, the Kimberley came late to the national park scene. Indeed, Australia's first national park, the Royal (just south of Sydney), was proclaimed in April 1879, some three months before Alexander Forrest became the first European to travel deeply into the interior of the Kimberley.

Six of the seven national parks of the Kimberley give visitors a good cross-section of the region and are generally accessible. The seventh, Drysdale River National Park, is situated in the northern section of the Kimberley Plateau, but access is extremely difficult.

With more than 30,000 visitors each year, Geikie Gorge is the most visited Kimberley national park, but it is Purnululu that has captured the public imagination. Many visitors prefer to take a flight over or into the park from Kununurra, Turkey Creek, Wyndham, Halls Creek and/or Broome, because the track to the Bungle Bungle Range remains a challenging 4WD experience. The other parks each have their own special appeal: Windjana Gorge and Tunnel Creek (which, with Geikie, are collectively known as the Devonian Reef National Parks), Mirima, which contains Hidden Valley, and Wolfe Creek Meteorite Crater.

Visitors to the Kimberley who visit as many of the national parks as possible see the very best of the landscape, plants, animal life and rock art the area has to offer. On a Kimberley map, "National Park" is the designation of an area of special interest and that stands out even in a region full of geographical oddities and wonderful scenery.

Purnululu

Purnululu or Bungle Bungle National Park was first declared in March 1987 and since that time has grown in size as more of the surrounding area has been added to the park. Purnululu now covers an area of 320,000 ha. The feature everyone comes to see is a sandstone range about 33 km long, 23 km wide and rising to 270 m above the plains.

It has been suggested that this park has the potential to attract as many visitors as Australia's most famous symbol of the outback, Uluru. Although the Bungle Bungle Range doesn't have the same solitary grandeur, it does provide an area of endless fascination: narrow gorges lined with tall *Livistona* fan palms, occasional isolated pools glowing golden in the sunlight reflected from rock walls, and everywhere the characteristic black-and-orange domes.

The rocks and canyons of Mirima National Park (opposite) create their own special environment. Once you enter the maze of canyons the silence can be complete, although this national park is within walking distance, just a few kilometres, of the township of Kununurra. The boabs and glowing rock walls found in this park are a memorable sight.

Reaching towards the sun, a group of young palm trees (above) fills the floor of a canyon in the Bungle Bungle Range. Some of the plants in the region of the Bungle Bungle have been discovered by botanists so recently that they have yet to be named. On the range itself, the most pervasive and spectacular is this unnamed species of *Livistona* fan palm.

We will probably never know when the first people came to the Purnululu area, however archaeologists have unearthed relics from 21,000 years ago downstream on the Ord River. It is likely that settlement was much earlier than that – perhaps as far back as 50,000 years. Certainly the Bungle Bungle Range was a significant feature for several Aboriginal groups at the time when the first European settlers arrived: the range is destined to prove a cultural treasure-trove of rock paintings and burial sites when a thorough archaeological exploration is carried out.

The first Europeans to see the Bungle Bungle Range were Alexander Forrest and his party in 1879. Looking towards the range, Forrest wrote: "To the north there was nothing promising, all rough and rangy." This opinion carried through to the next century of occupation: no matter how beautiful the spectacle, if cattle could not graze on it, the land was worthless.

"Stumpy" Michael Durack, later a partner in the nearby Lissadell station, was the first person to take out a lease that covered part of the Bungle Bungle Range. That was in 1881, but this lease lapsed in 1897. The unusual name was probably given to it by Arthur Muggleton, who leased it and nearby Tickalara station between 1929 and 1937. The name may have just been a product of Muggleton's whimsical humour, or it may have been a corruption of Purnululu, the Aboriginal name for the range, which simply means "sandstone". Another plausible explanation is the widespread occurrence of *Dicanthium fecundum* or "bundle bundle" grass and the accidental corruption of the spelling over time.

"Bungle Bungle station" subsequently became an out-station of Turner station and, after the Ord River was dammed in 1962, it was included in an area resumed as a regeneration reserve to rectify the results of previous overgrazing.

The area's current high profile was established after the Western Australian Department of Tourism assigned Roger Garwood, a Perth photographer, to photograph it in 1981. Two years later the Bungle Bungle Range featured in the *Wonders of WA* television series. In the 1996 dry season, about 14,500 people explored the range at ground level, while an estimated 25,000 flew over it.

An Aboriginal legend tells of a galah fighting with an echidna. As the galah attacked, the echidna frantically dug holes in an attempt to hide, thus forming the mounds and hollows of the Bungle Bungle Range. Finally, the echidna raised its quills to fend off the attacker but they all fell out. Those quills became the tall palm trees scattered about the Bungle Bungle.

As part of the planned and management approach to visitor access all recreational activity is restricted to the western and southern sides of the range – these areas are accessible from the main access track that connects the park to the Great Northern Highway. The western part is an area of tall cliffs and narrow gorges (such as Echidna Chasm), while the southern end, along Piccaninny Creek, has the banded domes for which the Bungle Bungle Range is famous. From the air, the most clearly distinguishable single feature is Piccaninny Gorge: a deep gash that almost cuts the main range in two.

Mysterious and surreal, the eroded sandstone ridges and domes of the Bungle Bungle Range (above) rise from the floodplains of the Ord River to cover 450 sq. km with hills riddled with creekbeds and gorges.

Geikie Gorge

When you travel by boat along the Fitzroy River where it passes through the Geikie Range, the most striking feature you see is the bands of colour in the rock in the gorge. It's like a layer cake: the rock directly above the river is a pale cream; above 15 m there is a distinct shift to an orange/grey, which extends skywards. The demarcation is the floodline, the height the water reaches when the Fitzroy changes from the sluggish stream of the dry season into the raging torrent of the Wet, draining an area half the size of Victoria at a rate of 27,300 cu. m per second. In the Wet, the public facilities area of the 3136 ha park does not host visitors: it is 7 m under water.

From the air, the Geikie, Napier and Oscar ranges still look a lot like the offshore reef they were 350 million years ago when they formed around the island that is now the Kimberley Plateau. The 6 km long gorge was formed as the Fitzroy River cut through the soft limestone. The effect today is spectacular: this special combination of river and rock (and the area's many birds, fish and crocodiles) attracts thousands of visitors every year.

Some of the fish found in the river hark back to the region's oceanic origins. Swordfish and stingrays, creatures normally associated with the seas and oceans, are sometimes found in the Fitzroy River at Geikie Gorge, more than 300 km from the coast. They have fully adapted to fresh water and live alongside the more typical river dwellers of the Kimberley; barramundi and freshwater crocodiles.

Geikie Gorge was named "Geikie Canyon" by Edward T. Hardman, the Western Australian Government Geologist, in 1883 in honour of the noted British geologist, Sir Archibald Geikie. It was a most fitting piece of nomenclature. The traditional owners of the area, the "Bunuba people", refer to the area as *darngku*.

Wolfe Creek Meteorite Crater

About 300,000 years ago, a lump of cosmic iron (which may have weighed up to 50,000 tonnes) collided with the Earth 150 km south of the present township of Halls Creek. This was no mere shooting star, disintegrating on contact with the atmosphere in a brief flash of fire. Our atmosphere hardly slowed this meteor down at all – it probably hit the ground at a speed of 100,000 km/h or more, forming a crater almost one kilometre across and around 150 m deep!

It has since been largely filled by shifting desert sands and today the rim is only 55 m above the interior and up to 35 m above the surrounding desert. Indeed, only low rainfall and a very slow erosion process have allowed the crater to remain so clearly recognisable. In a different climate area it could have become much less distinct.

The best perspective of the crater is obtained from the air, from where it appears as an enormous pockmark in the arid plain. Although the unusual formation had been noted by people on the ground, it was only after Dr Frank Reeves, a geologist, flew over the crater

Testimony to the volume and power of its floods, the walls of Geikie Gorge (opposite below) are bleached to heights of 15 m above the dry-season river level. During flood peaks, the Fitzroy River flows at the rate of a staggering 27,300 cu. m per second. At quieter times (opposite above) the river's banks here allow passage on foot.

A one-kilometre-wide bullseye in the desert (left), Wolfe Creek Meteorite Crater, the world's second largest crater from which meteor fragments have been recovered, was formed 300,000 years ago when a 50,000-tonne body struck at 100,000 km/h. The crater base retained its symmetry well, thanks to the region's arid conditions.

in June 1947 and later returned on a land expedition that the theory that it is a meteorite crater was widely accepted (although some geologists believe it to be of volcanic origin).

In fact, the Wolfe Creek Meteorite Crater is the Earth's second largest meteorite crater from which meteor fragments have been recovered. The much more recently formed Coon Butte Crater near Canyon Diablo in the North American State of Arizona is 1.6 km wide. Wolfe Creek itself is a small stream east of the 1460 ha park, which was named after Robert Tennant Stowe Wolfe, an early prospector and storekeeper in the region.

Windjana Gorge

The walls of Windjana Gorge rise abruptly from the wide alluvial floodplain of the Lennard River, reaching about 100 m high in some places. The 3.5 km long gorge cuts through the limestone of the Napier Range; part of an ancient barrier reef, which can also be seen at Geikie Gorge National Park.

Like Geikie Gorge and Tunnel Creek, Windjana Gorge is a cleft through a fossil reef. However, the Lennard River flows through Windjana Gorge only in the wet season: in the Dry, it is a series of deep, cool pools at the foot of high orange-grey cliffs. These cliffs, with deep grooves between the columns of limestone, give the impression of organ pipes. This effect has come about through the weathering of the limestone by small streams of water that have been sufficiently acidic to dissolve the chemically sensitive limestone.

Lush vegetation, including figs and river red gums, lines the banks of the river at the base of the cliffs but the top of the ridges have only sparse vegetation, principally tussock grass. There are generally harmless freshwater crocodiles living in the pools, along with a large fish population. The fish are the attraction for the numerous waterbirds that live in the 2134 ha

■ Around 20,000 visitors marvel at spectacular Windjana Gorge and its fissured cliffs (above) each year. Like Geikie Gorge, Windjana has been carved through a fossil reef, and its banks are lined with vegetation. During the Dry, the Lennard River (right), which formed the gorge, is a series of deep pools that attract numerous waterbirds and are home to freshwater crocodiles. To protect plant and animal life during the dry season, visitors are asked to stay on the designated paths, which feature signs describing the geology, flora and fauna.

A series of ponds under clear blue skies in the dry season, the Lennard River (left) gives no indication of its wet season force which has cut 4 km through the Napier Range to create 90 m high cliffs.

A damp, dark place inhabited by bats, Tunnel Creek (below) is made less daunting by a roof collapse that has created a natural skylight. The creek began as a fault line in the limestone of the Napier Range. Over millennia, water dissolved the rock to form the underground creek.

park during the Dry. These include herons and the large, stately black-necked stork or jabiru. On the 3.5 km track that winds through the gorge, visitors may see these and other wildlife, as well as the fossilised remains of earlier life forms held fast in its walls.

Tunnel Creek

Down the track between Windjana and Geikie gorges lies Tunnel Creek. Under the harsh sun that scorches the Kimberley, a visit to Tunnel Creek is a very unusual experience. This is a dark, damp place where visitors take a walk along a path under a limestone ridge. In some places, the 750 m path is dark and a torch is required. However, in the middle of the underground walkway is a bright place where sunlight streams through a hole in the roof of the cave. This is the result of the limestone roof collapsing after being undermined by the river. Tunnel Creek has taken the easiest path in its course along a fault line through the limestone. The most notable inhabitants of this 91 ha park are the five known species of bats that have taken up residence in the underground caverns. The freshwater crocodile is found here too but despite its reputation for avoiding people visitors should be vigilant.

Mirima

Not everyone is fortunate enough to explore Purnululu on foot. However, there is an easily accessible alternative that, while it may not be as extensive or impressive as the better-known site, still has the capacity to instil in the visitor a sense of wonder and a feeling for the banded sandstone towers of the Kimberley. Mirima National Park, previously

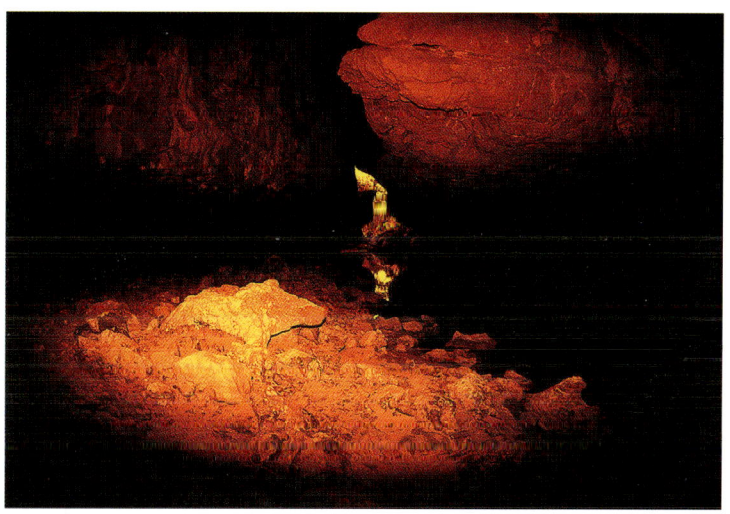

■ The ancient rock formations of the Mitchel River National Park (below) are characteristic of this north-western part of the Kimberley. Access to the park is still a challenge and a four-wheel-drive vehicle is essential. Despite the rigours of the trip, the opportunity to see some of the country's superb rock art draws more visitors each year.

known as Hidden Valley, which covers 2068 ha, is less than five minutes by car from the centre of Kununurra, yet within its narrow gorges, the only signs of civilisation are the graded tracks and picnic facilities. For those who have the time to simply sit and gaze about them this is a wonderful place. The sunlight playing on the ancient walls gives a constantly changing view of the rugged rock.

There are several boabs near the road within Hidden Valley. The more enthusiastic visitor can climb to the top of the ridge past the end of the road for a bird's-eye view over the northern part of Kununurra. It's a dramatic contrast. In one direction there's a modern, rural Australian service town, but as you retrace your steps into the glade, you are stepping into a scene that is as old as the ancient landforms around you.

Drysdale River

There are no gazetted access roads into Drysdale River National Park, a vast wilderness covering 448,264 ha in the north Kimberley. Indeed, the park was largely a biological unknown until a 1975 scientific expedition surveyed it and noted the great diversity of life including 594 different plants and all the native mammals one would expect to be present in the area. Some rare reptile species have been found in this isolated place and it is likely that many more may still be discovered. Scientists continue to discover rare or unusual species, including many reptiles that are found only in the park.

Drysdale River National Park, given the difficulty of access, looks set to remain an almost untouched example of the Kimberley landscape: a place of eucalypt forests and densely vegetated riverbanks and billabongs.

Mitchell River

The Mitchell River's course through sandstone country has created deep gorges and some spectacular waterfalls across the Mitchell Plateau in the Kimberley's far north-west. Access to the 115,000 ha Mitchell River National Park is a challenge at any time of year and a four-wheel-drive vehicle is essential. From the junction of Gibb River Road and Kalumburu Road, Mitchell Falls (*Punamii-unpuu*) is 172 km north of the Gibb River Road.

Remnants of rainforest cloak some parts of the plateau's ramparts but on the plateau itself there are open woodlands and broad valleys. This remote and beautiful place, the traditional home of the Kandijwal people, is still revealing its biological uniqueness. It also contains some extraordinary Aboriginal art sites, including the group known as the "Bradshaws". The wishes of the Kandijwal community, which exclude swimming below the falls or in the pools, are observed in the management of the area. The magnificent four-tiered falls are a memorable sight and sound, and a superb reward for the effort required to reach them. The final hour-long stretch must be done on foot but the spectacular view from the rim of some dramatic gorges along the way is a great incentive. A helicopter ride over the falls is a speedier alternative but a very different experience.

The Mitchell River (above) has its source on the plateau and, flowing through sandstone country, has cut deep gorges on its path to the sea at Walmesley Bay. During the wet season the numerous waterfalls along the river's course tumble off the plateau, continuing the process of erosion.

FAVOURITE PLACES IN THE KIMBERLEY

Broome

For anyone arriving in Broome after travelling west for days through some of the more remote areas of the Kimberley, the first glimpse of ocean is sure to stir the soul, raise a smile and have them reaching for their swimming costume! The sparse desert landscape disappears behind you as you reach the edge of the continent. Take a few days to unwind here and learn about the fascinating pearling industry that is an integral part of the town's history. July temperatures in the high 20s mean that for anyone wanting an ideal summer holiday in the cooler months, Broome is the perfect destination – you'll be able to relax on your own private stretch of the 22 km long Cable Beach. And if your visit coincides with a full moon, head for Roebuck Bay to witness the Staircase to the Moon, a natural phenomenon occurring when the exposed mudflats create the illusion of a staircase reaching up to the moon.

Gantheaume Point

Gantheaume Point offers the visitor to Broome a wonderful view across to Cable Beach. With sparse spinifex shrubland in the foreground, the contrast between the turquoise water and the pristine sand can be fully appreciated. It is here, too, that the Kimberley colours shine. Look around you and the vibrant red sandstone is without doubt the most

striking feature of Gantheaume Point. Rocky outcrops that taper out to meet the Indian Ocean display a colour combination that is simply breathtaking. The rocks at Gantheaume Point also enclose Anastasia's Pool, a small pool built by a former lighthouse keeper for his arthritic wife. The sandstone at the base of the cliff contains dinosaur footprints, believed to be those of a carnivorous species that lived 120 million years ago.

Lake Argyle

Lake Argyle, which reaches from the magnificent Carr Boyd Ranges in the west to the Northern Territory border in the east, is the result of an amazing feat of engineering. Formed in 1972 by the damming of the Ord River, it is Australia's largest man-made lake, covering an area of approximately 1000 sq. km – large enough to be classed as an inland sea. The bays, creeks and waterfalls of the shoreline are well worth exploring and the lake itself is dotted with islands. It has also developed its own ecosystems in which native flora and fauna abound. Fishing and canoeing are popular, but perhaps the best way to experience the area's magnificent scenery and wildlife is to take one of the many available boat cruises or, for those who prefer a bird's-eye view, a scenic flight over the lake offers an unforgettable experience.

Gibb River Road

Although it's possible to see the Kimberley without venturing onto the Gibb River Road, for a true outback experience and to see some of the Kimberley's most dramatically rugged scenery, travelling along at least part of this route is an absolute must. Originally constructed to transport cattle to the ports of Derby and Wyndham, the 660 km stretch of road remains largely unsealed and corrugations in its surface can make for a difficult drive. High clearance or 4WD vehicles are strongly recommended; conventional vehicles, lightweight 4WDs and the towing of caravans and trailers are not. Spectacular scenery unfolds as you traverse the heart of the Kimberley. And while it is crucial to plan your trip and take your time, you must also be prepared to let your plans fall by the wayside. You need to be prepared for everything when you venture into this part of the country.

Emma Gorge

Emma Gorge is part of the Cockburn Range and is one of the Kimberley's most spectacular gorges. A scenic, almost tropical 1.6 km (one way) walk to Emma Falls will take about an hour. The variety of bird life in the area becomes evident as you walk and the vegetation is constantly changing, from savannah woodland to Kimberley rainforest. Along the way, loose rocks and large boulders can be slippery at times and the trail is rated as moderately difficult; it's important to watch your footing. However there are opportunities to stop and quietly enjoy the grandeur of your surroundings along the way. The sheer red cliffs reach up some 120 m on either side of the trail and are an impressive and distinguishing feature of the gorge. These sandstone walls continue to the picturesque Emma Falls, enclosing the enticing waterhole at the base. The icy plunge pool provides the opportunity for a refreshing swim before making the return journey.

Bungle Bungle Range

The dramatic sandstone domes of the Bungle Bungle Range are one of the great natural wonders of the Australian outback. Despite having existed for more than 20 million years and having been known locally for thousands of years, the domes, with their spectacular horizontal bands of orange and grey, have only relatively recently become known more widely. In fact it was only in 1987 that the area was declared a national park (Purnululu). The unsealed road into the park is for 4WD vehicles only and, although only 55 km long, it takes around three hours to reach the Bungle Bungles after turning off the Great Northern Highway. Alternatively the amazing domes can be admired during a scenic flight over the area. Either way, a visit to Purnululu National Park will be a highlight of any trip to the Kimberley.

Dampier Peninsula

This remote and spectacular area stretching north of Broome to Cape Leveque offers the nature lover an experience to remember – unspoiled coastline and secluded holiday retreats in tranquil community settings. It provides travellers with the rare opportunity to witness the lifestyle of Peninsula people and to learn about their special relationship

with the land. In agreeing to share this unique experience, visitors must also agree to respect the Aboriginal land, the culture and the privacy of the local people throughout the Peninsula, but particularly where access is restricted.

Geikie Gorge

The mighty Fitzroy River carved its way through an ancient Devonian limestone reef, creating the spectacular Geikie Gorge. The result today is a particularly stunning gorge with tranquil waters and an abundance of aquatic and bird life, as well as freshwater crocodiles. At first glance it is the magnificent colours of the limestone that catch your eye – a distinct top layer of natural dark grey which against the blue sky is an impressive sight, and a very light grey below. Closer examination, made possible by joining one of the available boat trips, reveals so much more. Iron oxides in the limestone create a wonderfully intense orange throughout the dark grey. The light grey is interspersed with a delicate dusty pink. The light colour of the lower part of the gorge is the result of the annual flooding of the Fitzroy River.

Kununurra

Kununurra – the name is a local Aboriginal word meaning "meeting of big waters"– is the gateway to the east Kimberley. It is quite different from other towns in the Kimberley and worth exploring. Those arriving in town at the end of a Kimberley adventure will be struck by the picturesque vision of fertile soils, from which food crops grow in abundance. A modern town with a well developed infrastructure, Kununurra has plenty to offer visitors. For something a little different, head out to the Zebra Rock Gallery. The world's only known deposits of this ancient rock have been found near Kununurra and you can watch craftsmen transforming the rock into exquisite items. Many 4WD, cruise and flight operators are based in Kununurra, so it's also an ideal starting point for your exploration of the Kimberley.

Wolfe Creek Crater

Just 20 km off the Tanami Road and 150 km south of Halls Creek, Wolfe Creek Crater, with its astonishing symmetry and hidden interior, is a most surprising sight. A rocky but short climb takes you to the top of the rim and from there you'll see a series of perfect circular formations, much like a bullseye. The centre of the crater is thick with vegetation – a lush green patch in an otherwise dry landscape. Closer to the sides it is much like the surrounding countryside, with clumps of spinifex and a sparse scattering of trees. Over

time, wind-swept sands have largely filled the crater and today its base is only 20 m lower than the ground level outside. It is possible, though not recommended due to the loose, rocky surface, to venture down into the crater.

Mitchell River NP

The Mitchell River National Park offers a true Kimberley experience, which includes the opportunity to explore spectacular Mitchell Plateau and the thunderous Mitchell Falls. Covering an impressive area of 115,000 ha, the park is important not only as a wilderness area but also as a significant Aboriginal heritage site. Cascading waterfalls and rugged gorges carved by the Mitchell River and its tributaries border the plateau. Access is via a minor road branching off the Gibb River Road. The journey is not for the faint-hearted and visitors should allow themselves a few days for travel and to soak up the wonders of this beautiful, remote corner of the country.

El Questro

The intention of the brothers who claimed this land was that the name should describe a land of "great beauty and big mountains". Another interpretation could be paradise in the Kimberley, because that's what it feels like on arrival at this vast property off the Gibb River Road. Nestled alongside the Cockburn Range, the station was developed in 1991 to provide a unique Australian holiday destination. In this remote location El Questro offers four independent and completely different accommodation experiences: the internationally acclaimed homestead; tented cabins at Emma Gorge; family bungalows; and riverside camping. The range of activities includes horse-riding, barramundi fishing, exploring canyons and gorges on foot or by boat, and flights over some of the Kimberley's most spectacular features.

Windjana Gorge

A leisurely afternoon walk along the 4 km stretch of narrow limestone canyon that is the majestic Windjana Gorge offers a memorable experience. As you enter the gorge, the sound of screeching cockatoos overhead breaks the silence, but peace soon returns. Enormous, jagged, vertical cliffs of dark brown and grey surround you, but when the sun is low in the sky, a vibrant orange creeps into the limestone and creates faultless and dramatic mirror images of the cliffs in the water below. Freshwater crocodiles are found here and, in the cooler months, can be seen at close range basking in the sun on the banks of the gorge. A stunning array of flora and fauna, as well as the primeval life forms that have fossilised within the gorge walls, make this walk a "must-do". While in the Windjana Gorge NP, you will also have the chance to track down examples of Wandjina rock paintings.

Buccaneer Archipelago

The large group of islands to the north of Derby and King Sound is known widely as the Buccaneer Archipelago but it is often referred to as the "Thousand Islands". A coastal area unequalled in its beauty, the archipelago can be marvelled at from the sea or the

air. A cruise that includes a visit to Cockatoo Island is sure to be the experience of a lifetime – whirlpools formed by massive tides have to be seen to be believed, as does the unusual Horizontal (or "two-way") Waterfall at Talbot Bay. Back on land, rugged red cliffs and secluded white beaches provide a perfect place in which to unwind.

Elgee Cliffs

The Kimberley is so vast that one can only get a good overview from the air. Fortunately, you will find sightseeing operations at most airstrips in the region. One of the most remarkable sights in the Kimberley is Elgee Cliffs, a dramatic landform on the western bank of

the Chamberlain River not far from El Questro Wilderness Park. The cliffs escarpment is 125 km long, one of the most spectacular geological formations in Australia and one that is best appreciated from the air. For the earth-bound there are some 4WD tracks to the cliffs from the base at El Questro.

Five Rivers Lookout

Venturing up to Wyndham's Five Rivers Lookout, particularly if it can be done to coincide with either the sunrise or sunset, is a rewarding experience. The drive to the top is short but steep, however once the few hairpin bends have been safely negotiated, the view is breathtaking. The confluence of five rivers – the Ord, Forrest, Pentecost, Durack and King – as they flow into Cambridge Gulf, is an impressive sight. The lookout is on the highest point of the Bastion Range which forms the backdrop to the town of Wyndham, and provides a spectacular view through almost 360 degrees. As well as the sweeping, distant views you'll notice the images, closer below, of mangrove swamps, mudflats, hills and ridges that surround the rivers. And the sight of Wyndham Port directly below is a reminder of the importance of Wyndham in the development of the Kimberley.

TRAVEL DOSSIER

Travelling to the Kimberley

The prefix for all West Australian telephone numbers is 08.

By air: Qantas provides a regular air service into Broome with connecting flights from Perth and the eastern States via Alice Springs. Qantas also has a regular air service into Darwin from most major Australian ports.
www.qantas.com.au
Skipper Aviation operates between Broome and Derby. (08) 9192 2887
Airnorth provides a regular regional air service that links Broome and Kununurra to Darwin. www.airnorth.com.au
Virgin Blue provides a regular service to Broome from Brisbane, Sydney, Melbourne and Adelaide.
www.virginblue.com.au
Visitors to the region can also access a number of local charter operators who provide regular transport services to some town centres within the Kimberley as well as scenic charter flights.
By coach: Greyhound-Pioneer services all major Kimberley towns daily from Perth and Darwin. www.greyhound.com.au
McCafferty's regularly services all major Kimberley towns.
www.mccaffertys.com.au
Australia-wide phone numbers:
Qantas. 13 13 13

Airnorth: 1800 627 474
Virgin: 13 67 89
Travel Coach Australia (National Reservation Centre for McCafferty's and Greyhound Pioneer):13 20 30
By car: The distances from Kununurra to the following cities by road are

Darwin:	827 km
Perth:	3214 km
Brisbane:	3538 km
Sydney:	4247 km
Melbourne:	3557 km
Adelaide:	2924 km

Broome to Kununurra is 1040 km.
Motoring information, maps and WA accommodation guide are available from the RAC of WA, 228 Adelaide Terrace, Perth WA 6000. Freecall 1800 807 011.
www.rac.com.au/travel
Rental cars: Rental vehicles, 4WD or standard, are available in Broome, Derby, Wyndham, Halls Creek and Kununurra.

Tour operators

Land: Tours are conducted in and from Kununurra, Halls Creek, Fitzroy Crossing, Derby and Broome.
Sea: There are a number of cruises and vessels available for charter. Bookings can be made at Broome, Derby, Wyndham, Kununurra and Fitzroy Crossing. Contact regional tourist bureaus for the latest information.

Air: Commercial operators run scenic flights from the airports of Broome, Derby, Fitzroy Crossing, Halls Creek, Wyndham and Kununurra. Float planes and helicopters can be chartered at Kununurra and Broome, helicopters in Derby and scenic helicopter flights operate from Turkey Creek Roadhouse.

Tourist information

Information about the Kimberley and holiday bookings are available from:
WA **Visitor Centre**
Cnr Wellington St and Forrest Place, Perth WA 6000.
For the cost of a local call: 1300 361 351.
Fax: (08) 9481 0190
www.westernaustralia.net
Broome Visitor Centre
Broome Rd, Cnr Bagot Street
Broome WA 6725.
Ph. (08) 9192 2222
www.ebroome.com/tourism
Derby Visitor Centre
2 Clarendon St, Derby 6728.
Ph. (08) 9191 1426
Freecall: 1800 621 426
www.derbytourism.com.au
Halls Creek Tourist Information Centre
Hall Street, Halls Creek 6770.
Ph. (08) 9168 6262
Fax (08) 9168 6467

Kununurra Tourist Bureau
Coolibah Dr., Kununurra 6743.
Ph. (08) 9168 1177 Fax (08) 9168 2598
www.eastkimberley.com
Wyndham Tourist Information Centre
Kimberley Motors (Mobil)
6 Great Northern Hwy, Wyndham 6740.
Ph. (08) 9161 1281
Fitzroy Crossing Tourist Bureau
Flynn Drive, Fitzroy Crossing 6765.
Ph. (08) 9191 5355 Fax (08) 9191 5085

Accommodation

Broome: Broome Seashells Resort; Cable Beach Club Resort; Mangrove Hotel; Mercure Inn-Continental Broome; Palms Resort; Roebuck Bay Hotel/Motel; The Kimberley Klub (Backpackers); Tropicana Inn.
Derby: Derby Boab Inn; Goldsworthy Connection; King Sound Resort Hotel; Spinifex Hotel; West Kimberley Lodge; Willare Bridge Roadhouse (57 km south of town on Great Northern Hwy).
Fitzroy Crossing: Crossing Inn; Fitzroy River Lodge.
Halls Creek: Halls Creek Motel; Kimberley Hotel; Old Halls Creek Lodge.
Warmun Community: Turkey Creek Roadhouse (1 km north of community).
Wyndham: Gulf Breeze Guest House; Wyndham Community Club; Wyndham Town Hotel.

Kununurra; Country Club; Desert Inn; Duncan House (bed and breakfast); Hotel Kununurra; Kimberley Court; Kununurra Backpackers; Lake Argyle Inn; Lakeside Resort; Mercure Inn.

Caravan parks and camping grounds are in all the above towns and at Turkey Creek Roadhouse. Several stations along the Kalumburu and Gibb River roads now offer accommodation, camping fuel, etc. A guide to these can be bought at the Derby Visitor Centre.

Station stays

Beverley Springs; Drysdale River; Ellenbrae; El Questro Wilderness Park; Kachana; Mt Elizabeth; Theda; Mt Hart Homestead.

Wilderness experience

Eco Beach, Cape Villaret; Kimberley Coastal Camp; Kooljaman, Cape Leveque; Lombadina Aboriginal Corp; Nature's Hideaway, Middle Lagoon; The Bushcamp, Faraway Bay.

Aboriginal communities

Some communities offer camping, supplies and guided tours but visiting a community may require a permit. Contact Dept of Indigenous Affairs, PO Box 7770, Cloisters Sq. Perth 6850. Ph. (08) 9235 8000 or toll free in WA 1300 651 077

Dining out

There are restaurants or cafes in all the towns with accommodation. In general, meals in the Kimberley are slightly more expensive than their equivalent in more populated, accessible areas of Australia, an inevitable result of the distance from supply centres.

National parks

The Kimberley regional office of the Department of Conservation and Land Management is at Messmate Way, Kununurra. PO Box 942, Kununurra, 6743. Ph. (08) 9168 0200, Fax (08) 9168 2179. Nature Base website: www.calm.wa.gov.au

Shopping

Broome: pearls, Argyle diamonds; Kununurra: Argyle diamonds, zebra stone jewellery; Derby: decorative sandstone ornaments from Kimberley Colourstone; Wyndham: crocodile-skin products from the Crocodile Farm. Carved boab nuts are available in several towns.

Aboriginal art

There are specialist shops in Broome, Derby, Fitzroy Crossing and Kununurra. Alternatively, visit some of the Aboriginal communities including Lombadina and One Arm Point on the Dampier Peninsula, where local art and artefacts are for sale. Shops selling Aboriginal art include:
Mac's Art Shop, Paspaley Plaza Shopping Centre, Broome. Ph/fax (08) 9192 7272.
Art Thingz, Kanagae Drive, Broome. Ph. (08) 9193 7103
Waringarri Aboriginal Arts, Speargrass Rd, Kununurra. Ph. (08) 9168 2212

Time

Western Australian time is two hours behind Eastern Standard Time and one and a half hours behind Central Standard Time. There is no daylight saving.

Clothing

Dress in the Kimberley tends to be very informal. Jackets and ties are rarely required. Shorts are generally acceptable.

Banking

Broome: ANZ, full branch, ATM; Bankwest, full branch, ATM; Challenge (Westpac), full branch, ATM; Commonwealth, full branch, ATM.
Derby: ANZ, full branch, ATM; agencies of Commonwealth and Bankwest.
Fitzroy Crossing: Agencies of ANZ and Commonwealth.
Halls Creek: Agencies of Bankwest and Commonwealth.
Wyndham: Agencies of Commonwealth and Bankwest.

Kununurra: Bankwest, full branch, ATM; Commonwealth, full branch, ATM.

Photography

Kimberley sunlight is very strong, so as a general rule you can use slow film. Avoid photographing subjects in part shade and part sun because the shade will turn out very dark and the well-lit parts too bright. This can be avoided in portraits by using a flash to "fill in" the shadows.

Quarantine regulations

Western Australia is free of many pests and diseases that plague other States and it is against the law to take some agricultural products into the State, fresh fruit and vegetables among them. Quarantine regulations are strictly enforced. There is a checkpoint 40 km east of Kununurra on Victoria Highway, then at the Western Australia-Northern Territory border. Mobile checkpoints may also operate on other entry roads. Information on the regulations may be obtained from the Katherine Visitors Centre, or the Timber Creek Hotel, 200 km north-east of Kununurra. A summary of import conditions appears on the WA Department of Agriculture website: www.agric.wa.gov.au or Ph. 1800 084 881.

INDEX

Acknowledgements

2003 edition

Special thanks for assistance with the fully revised (2003) edition.

Chris Done and Allen Grose, CALM; Kristie Dunn, Kimberley Land Council, Ron Rudolphy, Kimberley School of the Air; Dr Stephen Langford, Royal Flying Doctor Service; Bill Downey and Kevin Smith, Bureau of Meteorology; Ian Dickins, Fitzroy Crossing Tourist Bureau; Petra Meyer, Derby Visitor Centre; Geoff Vivian, Halls Creek Tourist Information Centre; Gina Rockett, Kununurra Tourist Bureau; Lorre Daniel, Wyndham Tourist Information Centre and the staff at Broome Visitor Centre.

Previous editions

The revision editor (1998) would like to thank Cockatoo Island Resort, Jon Berry, Kimberley Development Commission, Mick Buckley, Pearl Producers Association, Joe Sherrard of Agriculture WA, Kostas Metaxas of Paspaley Pearls, Barry Hanstrum of the Bureau of Meteorology, Alison Quinn of the Broome Tourist Bureau, Derby Tourist Bureau, Fitzroy Crossing Tourist Bureau, Halls Creek Tourist Information Centre, Wyndham Tourist Information Centre, Kununurra Tourist Bureau, Kimberley Tourism Association, the RAC of WA Touring Department, Telstra Corporate Affairs WA, Viv Maitland of the RFDS, Wendy Albert of the Kimberley Bookshop, Peter Young of Ansett Australia, Denis Callaghan of the Aboriginal Affairs Department, Koolyanobbing Iron and the staff of many other businesses and tourist information centres.

The editor (1990) would like to thank the people of the Kimberley who gave their time unstintingly, providing information and assistance during the research process and in checking the manuscript. In particular thanks must go to Chris Done, regional manager of CALM, the MacDonald family of Fossil Downs, Dame Mary Durack Miller, the WA Tourism Commission, the shire councils of the region, Ian Elliot, who checked the nomenclature.

Picture credits

Position of photographs on the page: *t* = top; *b* = bottom; *l* = left; *r* = right.

All photographs by Robbi Newman except the following: Kim Akerman 44 *b*, 46; Bill Bachman 97; Battye Library 37; Hugh Brown 2, 18, 26, 33 *b*, 56 *t*, 68, 77 *t*, 78 *t*, 81 *b*, 82, 100, 102, 104 *b*, 105, 106 *t* and *b*, 108, 109 *t* and *b*, 113, 114, 115, 116, 117 *t* and *b*, 118, 120, 122, 124 *t* and *b*, 128, 129 *t* and *b*, 134 *r*, 135 *b*, 136, 137, 138, 139 *t*; Bureau of Meteorology 31 *b*; Michael Cusack 98 *b*; Hazel de Berg (courtesy National Library of Australia) 61; Ken Eastwood 62; David Hancock 31 *t*; Kimberley Land Council 39; Kimberley School of the Air 69; Mike Langford 83 *t*; David McGonigal 3, 9, 12, 13, 22, 24, 40, 53 *b*, 59 *t*, 66 *b*, 71 *t*, 74, 88 *t* and *b*, 93 *t*, 103, 107, 110 *t* and *b*, 111, 121, 123 *t* and *b*, 125, 130, 134 *l*, 141, 142, 144 *t* and *b*, 146 *t* and *b*; Dame Mary Durack Miller 56 *b*; Mitchell Library, State Library of NSW 48 *b*, 51, 52 *l*, 53 *t*; NASA 33; National Library Of Australia 54, 60 *t*, 70 *b*; National Library Of Australia, Rex Nan Kivell Collection 71 *b*, 50 *l* and *r*, 52 *l* and *r*, 55; News Limited 3; Nick Rains front cover, 1, 138; Dick Smith 8, 10, 59 *b*, 67, 70 *t*, 84, 126, 131, 133, 135 *t*, 139; *b*, 147 *t*, 148, 149; Pip Smith 16 *b*, 98 *t*; Richard Thwaites 98 *t*; State Library of Victoria 40 *t*; Murray Spence 49, 77 *b*; Howard Whelan back cover, 4-5.

Further Reading

Dean Houston and others: *Bungle Bungle Range, Purnululu National Park, East Kimberley, Western Australia – a guide to the rocks, landforms, plants, animals and human impact.*

Mary Durack: *Kings in Grass Castle, Sons in the Saddle, The Rock and the Sand.*

Ion L. Idriess: *Outlaws of the Leopolds, Over the Range, One Wet Season.*

Hugh Edwards: *Port of Pearls* and *Kimberley: Dreaming to Diamonds.*

Georg Walter PSM: *Australia: Land, People, Mission.*

J.R.B. Love: *Stone Age Bushmen of Today.*

Ambrose Mungala Chalarimeri: *The man from the sunrise side.*

David Mowaljarlai and Jutta Malnic: *Yorro Yorro: everything standing up alive: Spirit of the Kimberley.*

Cathie Clement and Peter Bridge: *Kimberley Scenes: Sagas of Australia's last frontier.*

Peter Bridge: *Russian Jack.*

Malcolm Douglas: *Follow the Sun.*

Michael and Susan Cusack: *Our Year in the Wilderness.*

Ron and Viv Moon: *The Kimberley – An Adventurer's Guide.*

Rod Dickson: *The Price of a Pearl.*

Kevin F. Kenneally, Daphne Choules Edinger and Tim Willing. *Broome and Beyond: Plants and People of the Dampier Peninsula, Kimberley, WA.*

Stuart Garrow: *Big Tide Country: Kimberley tides and tidal life.*

Alasdair McGregor and Quentin Chester: *The Kimberley: Horizons of stone.*

Bernie Aquilina and William Reed: *Lure of the Pearl: Pearl Culture in Australia.*

Paul Marshall (ed.): *Raparapa Kularr Martuwarra: Stories from the Fitzroy River Drovers*

Banjo Woorunmurra and Howard Pederson: *Jandamarra and the Bunuba Resistance.*

Peter Burke: *The Drowning Dream.*

Di Morrissey: *Tears of the Moon, The Songmaster, Kimberley Sun.*

Edna Eckford Quilty: *Nothing Prepared Me!*

Bruce Shaw: *Countrymen, Bush Time Station Time, Banggaiyerri.*

Neville W Tickner: *Last of the Packhorse Stockmen.*

Tim Willing and Kevin Kenneally (eds): *Under a Regent Moon.*

Anne Marie Ingham: *Pioneers of the Kimberley: The Maggie Lilly Story.*

Veronica Ryan (ed.) *from digging sticks to writing sticks: Stories of Kija women.*

JS Battye Library of West Australian History: *Select Bibliography of the Natural History of the Kimberley Region of Western Australia.*

Cathie Clement: *A Guide to Printed Sources for the History of the Kimberley Region of Western Australia.*

Beryl Craig: *Kimberley Region: An Annotated Bibliography.*

Pat Lowes: Pat Lowe: *The Boab Tree; Jilji: Life in the Great Sandy Desert, Hunters and Trackers of the Australian Desert.*

I. Crawford: *We won the victory: Aborigines and outsiders on the north west coast of the Kimberley*

J. Doring, and others: *Gwion Gwion.*

G. Walsh: *Bradshaw Art of the Kimberleys, Bradshaws: Ancient Rock Paintings of North-west Australia.*